JAMES GORDANEER A Life In Painting

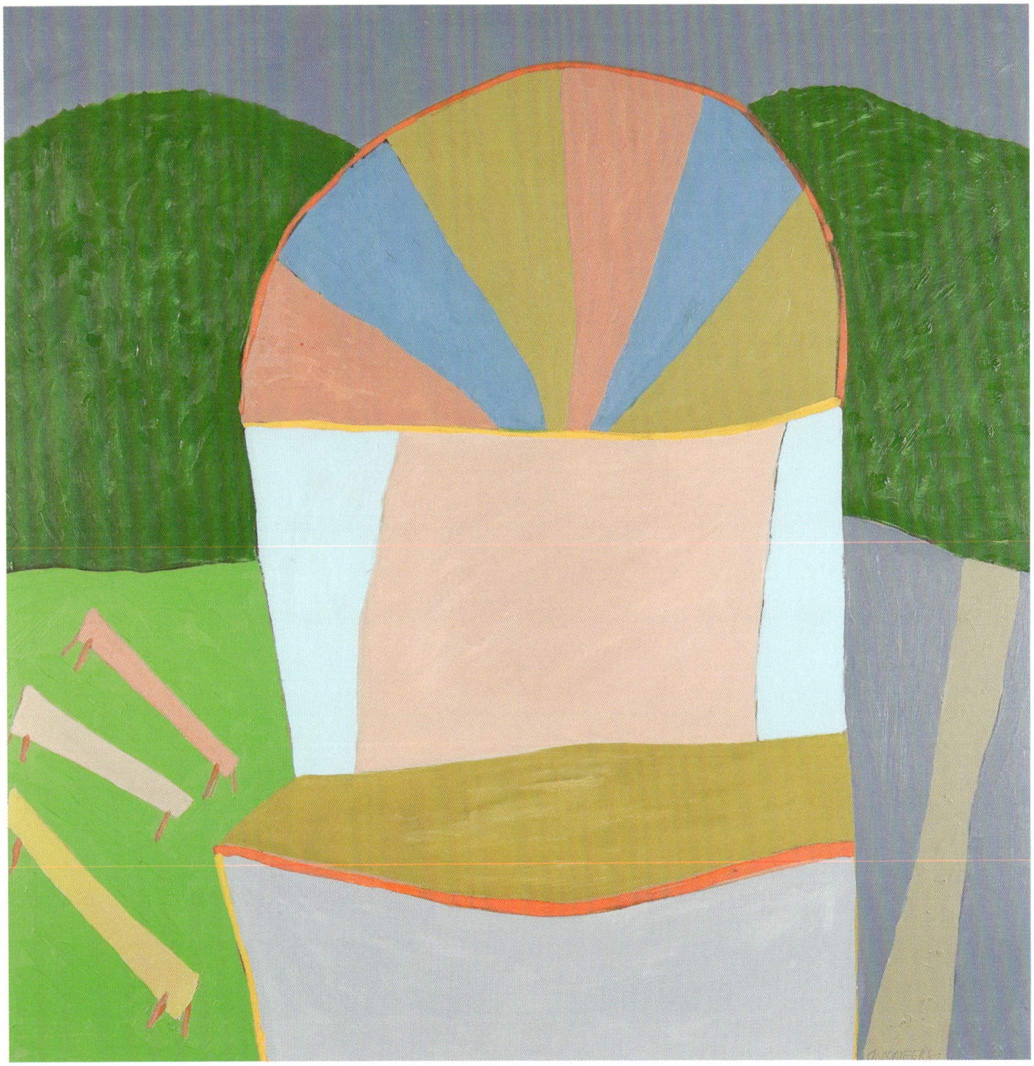

JAMES GORDANEER A Life In Painting

Lisa Baldissera & Nicole Stanbridge

ART GALLERY OF GREATER VICTORIA

Library and Archives Canada Cataloguing in Publication

Baldissera, Lisa, 1966–
James Gordaneer : a life in painting / Lisa Baldissera,
Nicole Stanbridge.

Includes bibliographical references and index.
Catalogue of an exhibition held at the Art Gallery of Greater Victoria,
Victoria, B.C., from April 6 – June 6, 2010.

ISBN 978-0-88885-358-5

1. Gordaneer, James—Exhibitions.
I. Gordaneer, James II. Stanbridge, Nicole, 1976-
III. Art Gallery of Greater Victoria IV. Title.

ND249.G67A4 2010 759.11 C2010-900340-3

COVER: **Send in the Clowns** (detail), 2009, oil on panel

TITLE PAGE: **Beacon Hill Series: Band Stand**, 1987, oil on panel

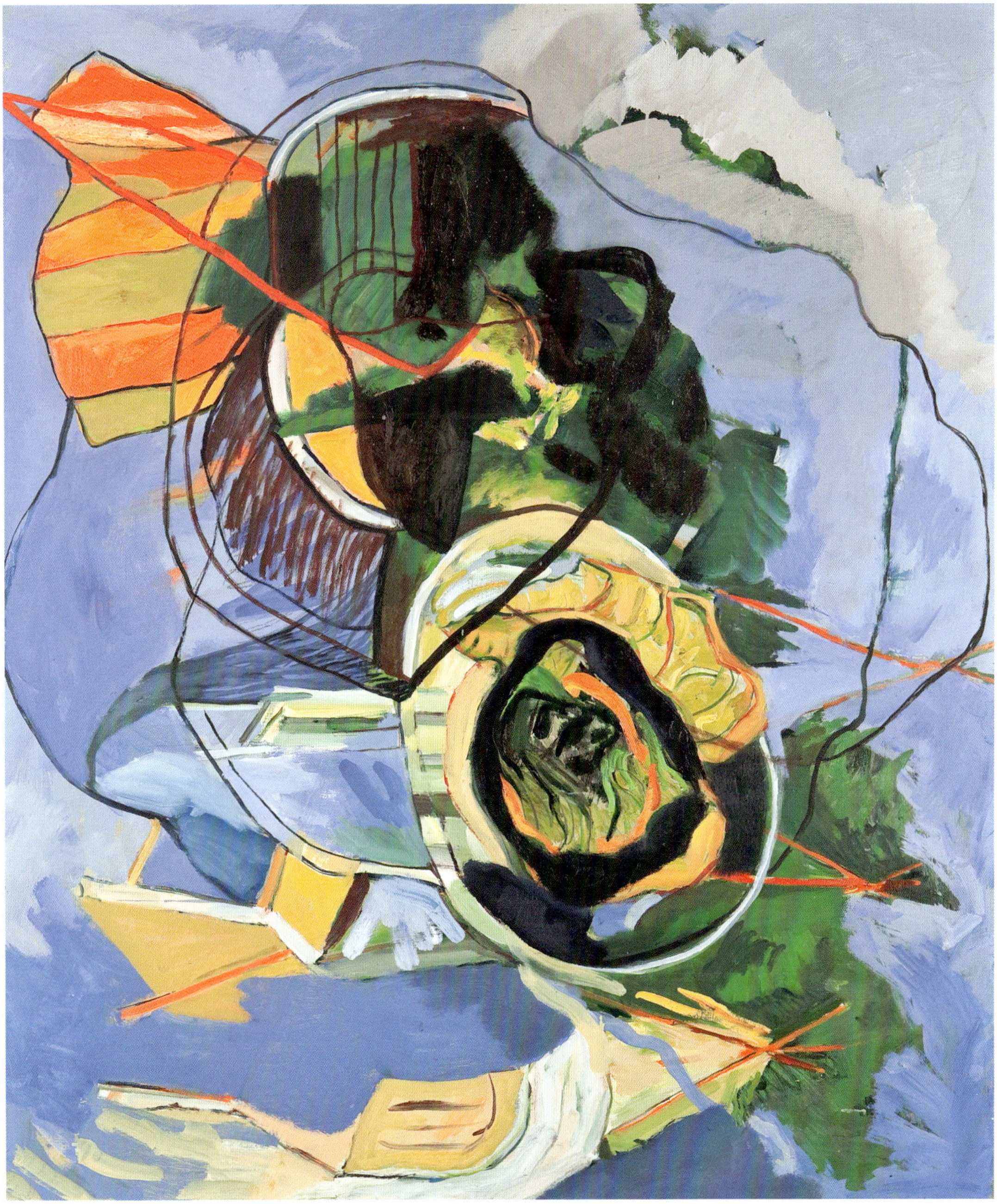

Summer Sky, Deep Woods, 2009, oil on panel

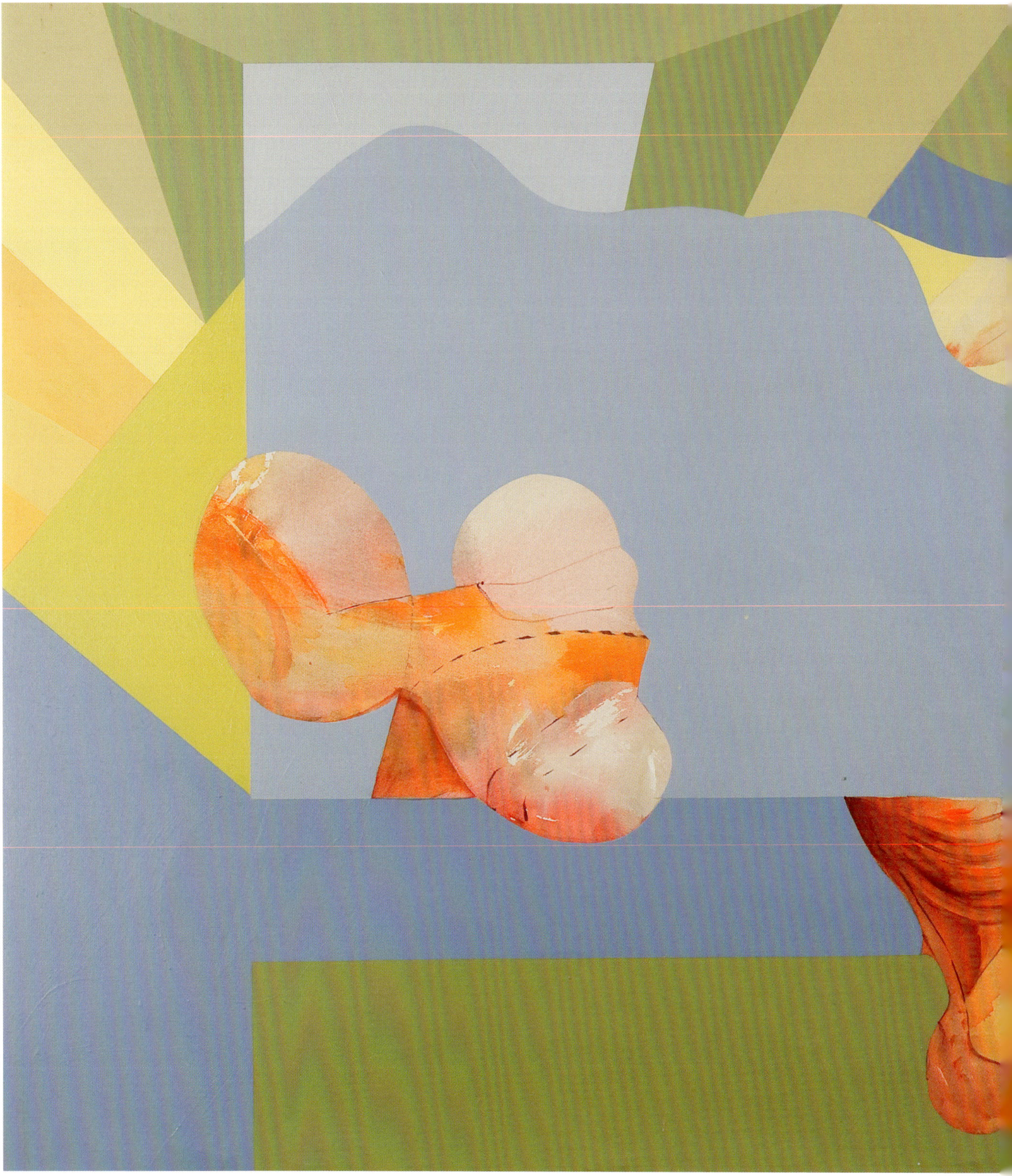

Contents

Sofa, 1971, oil on canvas

Director's Foreword

This publication documents the art of James Gordaneer, recognized as one of the most prolific painters in the Capital Region of British Columbia. The works in the book and the associated exhibition at the Art Gallery of Greater Victoria record a practice that has been extraordinarily active for almost six decades. They reveal a body of work remarkably consistent in its approach to form and colour as it moves between painterly abstraction and representation. Over his impressive career, Gordaneer has engaged in dialogue with many genres, including portraiture, landscape and still life, making his work difficult for art historians but a delight for the general public.

Born in southern Ontario, Gordaneer travelled extensively before settling in Victoria in 1976. As an instructor, he has been a positive influence on several generations of artists with his solid individualism and persistent determination. He serves as a link between many groups of artists active on southern Vancouver Island.

Gordaneer's work is held in many public collections, including the Canada Council Art Bank; McMichael Canadian Art Collection; Sarnia Art Gallery; Robert McLaughlin Gallery; Art Gallery of Peel; Leonard & Bina Ellen Art Gallery, Concordia University; Agnes Etherington Art Centre, Queen's University; Tom Thomson Memorial Art Gallery; Maltwood Art Museum and Gallery, University of Victoria; Homer Watson Gallery in Kitchener, Ontario; Toronto Dominion Bank Collection; and Art Gallery of Greater Victoria, as well as many private collections.

On behalf of the board and staff of the AGGV, I gratefully acknowledge the support of the BC Arts Council, the Canada Council for the Arts and the Capital Regional District. A special thanks to our exhibition sponsor, The Associates of the Art Gallery of Greater Victoria, which has so generously supported this project. The Associates' ongoing engagement with and dedication to the Gallery is highly valued. I also thank the Gordaneer family for their assistance and support, and Lynda and Alan Cassels for the loan of artwork from their collection. The idea for the publication and exhibition came from Lisa Baldissera, who was responsible for much of the research; her contribution is greatly appreciated. I wish to also thank the curator, Nicole Stanbridge, for her commitment and her enthusiasm for the project. Finally, and most importantly, thank you to James Gordaneer for sharing his remarkable work with all of us.

Jon Tupper
Director

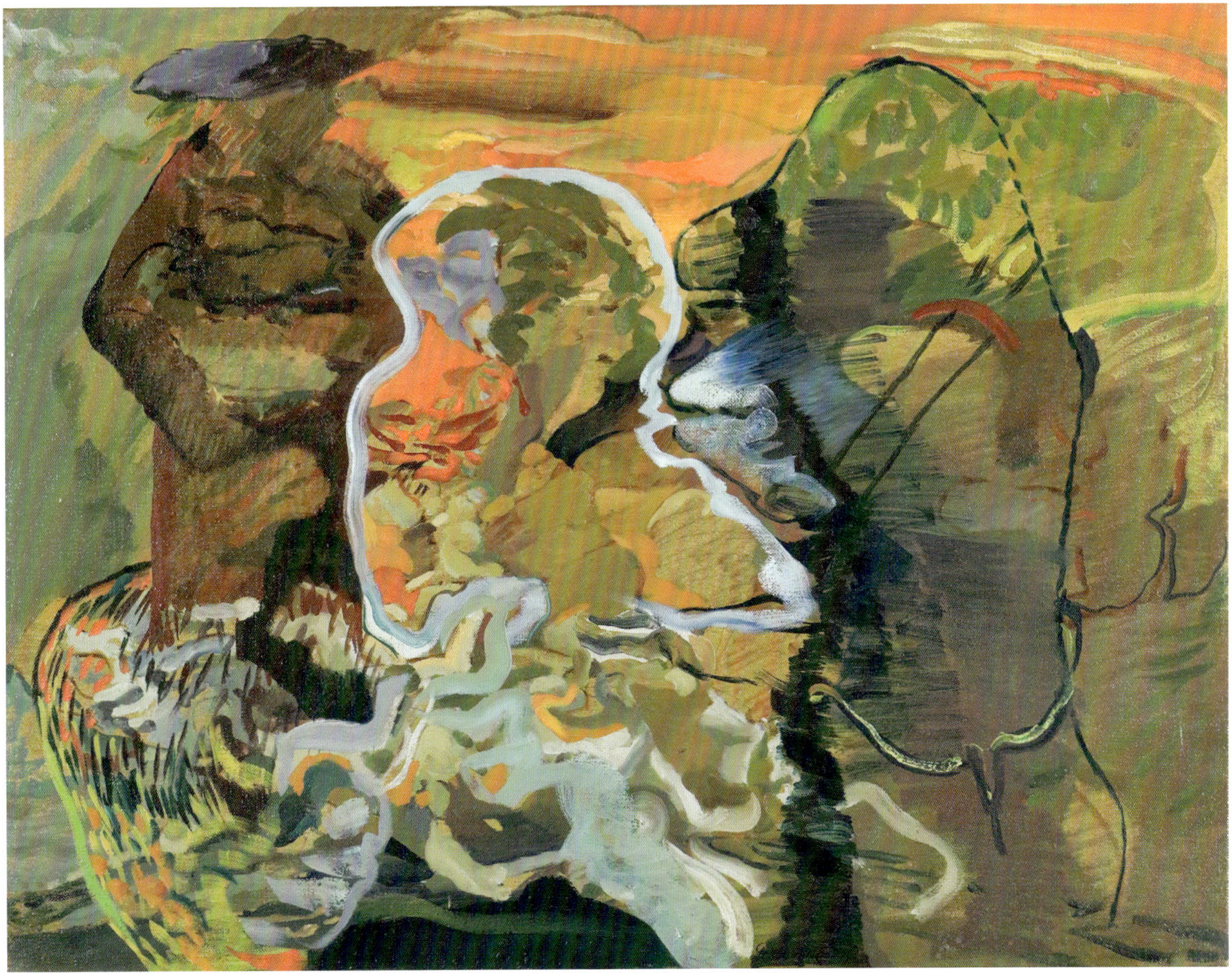

Arbutus Cove, 1978, oil on linen

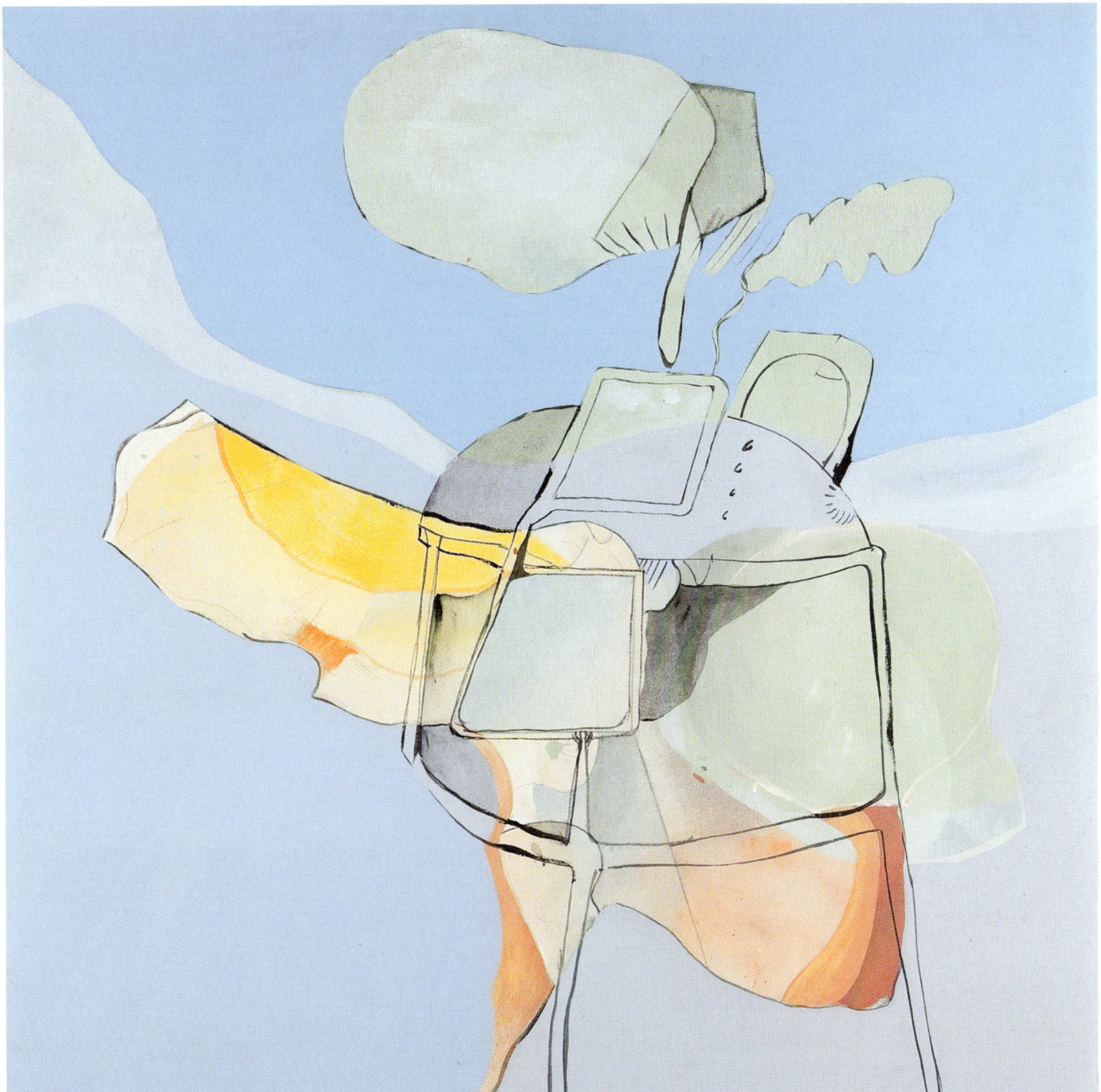

Space Odyssey, 1972, oil on linen

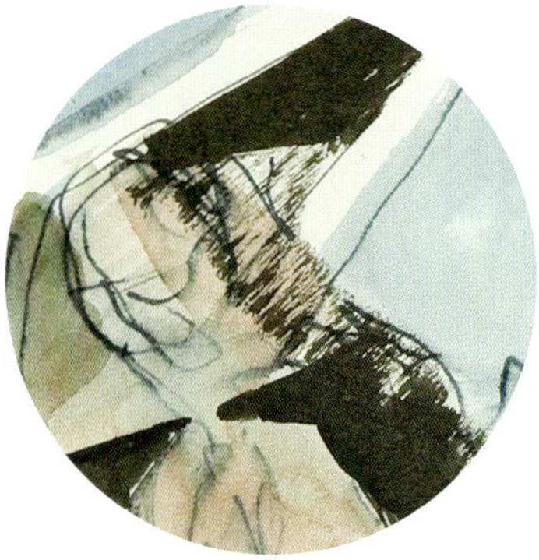

James Gordaneer: A Life in Painting

NICOLE STANBRIDGE

JAMES GORDANEER IS, IN THE TRUEST SENSE, an artist's artist and has been an integral part of the art community in Victoria since the 1970s. He is impressively prolific in his ever-evolving practice as he continually seeks out inspiration and motivation through dialogue with students and fellow artists. Whether sketching *en plein air* or painting in his studio, the act of art making is central to his life.

As a young man, he knew that art would play a major role in the choices he would make. However, the path Gordaneer took does not set itself conveniently in one art historical narrative. He has consciously resisted classification by refusing immersion in any one theory. While he has always remained cognizant of the dialogues taking place within Canadian and international art movements, he chooses to be selective in what he draws from those sources, creating his own unique visual vocabulary. The exploration of the process of painting has been Gordaneer's driving force. His curious nature was instrumental in challenging creative boundaries and setting a broader definition for his painting. His focus and unwavering drive to learn from his own art practice and that of his peers in the community are what bring such depth to the work he produces.

Delighting in the Act

James Gordaneer was born in Toronto in 1933. As a teenager he left school in grade nine and started working at a local grocery store in Toronto's east end. There came a point when he knew a more meaningful creative pursuit was out there to be discovered, and in 1952 he enrolled in summer courses at the Doon School of Fine Art. Over the next three years he had the opportunity to learn from artists such as Jock Macdonald, Carl Schaefer and Yvonne Housser, who taught him the value of painting and gave him the foundation he needed to confidently set his career in motion.

Gordaneer's studies at Doon were the extent of his formal art education. At the same time, he set off on a journey taken by many artists before him, travelling the world in search of new visions for his work. Late in 1955, Gordaneer left for San Miguel de Allende in Mexico.

A year prior, one of his instructors, Jack Bechtel, had travelled to Mexico, and he encouraged this young aspiring artist to follow in his path. Gordaneer's visits to San Miguel de Allende gave him the opportunity to learn from a new group of established and senior artists who suggested alternatives to the traditional landscape painting techniques he had become familiar with during his time at Doon. San Miguel de Allende was the site of one of the first art schools in Latin America, Bellas Artes, which Gordaneer attended for a short time. During his brief time studying in Mexico, he worked with fellow Canadian and Royal Canadian Academy of Arts member Leonard Brooks and Argentinean-American artist James Pinto.

During the 1950s, Gordaneer travelled throughout Europe and discovered the work of old masters and new revolutionaries while visiting major museums and galleries in France, Spain and Greece. In lieu of a formal education, these trips were instrumental to his development as an artist, bringing him into contact with established artists who inspired him to persevere in his endeavours as a painter. Despite his reservations about pursuing an institutional education, he was intrigued by the current dialogue regarding modernism, surrealism and abstract expressionism. In 1959, while in Buffalo, New York, Gordaneer was able to see first-hand how artists like Arshile Gorky, Willem de Kooning and Franz Kline were finding new ways to broaden the scope of painting. In the work of Gorky and de Kooning he recognized the modernist struggle between representation and abstraction that appealed to him. Likewise, Gordaneer has resisted modernist ideals of purity in abstraction and exclusivity of form. He also found resonance in the way Kline used brush strokes and lines to accurately reflect the expressiveness of a gesture or movement. In its abstraction and gestural vigour, Gordaneer's work from the 1970s, as well as his most recent work, demonstrates these influences. Despite his affinity for the aesthetic of the abstract expressionists, Gordaneer had the ability to keep a healthy distance from any one theory or style of painting. He assimilated everything he was exposed to and rearticulated the information in a way that worked for his sensibility as an artist.

Gordaneer sustained his travels throughout the 50s and early 60s as a part-time instructor at institutions in Toronto and surrounding areas. In 1961 he married and set off on another year of travel with his wife, Miria. On their return in 1962, he made the decision to leave the Toronto art scene for a new home in an abandoned schoolhouse in Orangeville, Ontario, just an hour northwest of the city. He had been exhibiting in Toronto and developing momentum in his career, but he wanted a change from the pace of the city. The move to a more rural setting gave him the space and resources to continue painting. Although he moved geographically out of the centre of artistic activity, he was becoming more connected to a broader community of artists through his membership in the Canadian Group of Painters, the Ontario Society of Artists and the Royal Canadian Academy of Arts, to which he was elected in 1973. At this point he had the means to focus on his practice and create a solid base for his family that would serve him well in the long run.

After several years of rural life, which he spent renovating the schoolhouse, starting a family and working through the concepts that had informed his work thus far, he was keen to connect with fresh artistic views. In the summer of 1976, Gordaneer and his family headed for the West Coast and set down roots in Victoria, British Columbia. The move provided Gordaneer with teaching opportunities and the new community of artists for which he had been looking. The year he arrived, he began teaching at Camosun College, a position he held for three years. At the suggestion of his colleague Jack Wise, he also became an instructor at the recently established Victoria College of Art. Gordaneer developed a close relationship with Wise, who was a prominent artist in Victoria. He truly valued his connection to his peers and students, but he did not want to be consumed by teaching. He made an effort to dedicate as much time as he could to the expansion of his own practice.

In 1987, after Gordaneer's first decade in Victoria, the Art Gallery of Greater Victoria presented an exhibition of work from his *Circus Series*. This series was produced after an experimental year in the early 1980s during which Gordaneer explored hard edge painting at the Victoria College of Art. The modernist aesthetic of hard edge painting and its purity of form and abstraction did not resonate with him, and the *Circus Series* was an attempt to find his way back to the painterly style that distinguished his work in the 1970s. As was his way when presented with a new style, Gordaneer assimilated some aspects of hard edge painting; the geometry and privileging of form and colour found its way into his work in the mid to late 1980s.

Shortly after this series, Gordaneer began a decade-long exploration into a new realm of painting. In 1989 he co-founded the Chapman Group of Artists with his collaborator Raymond

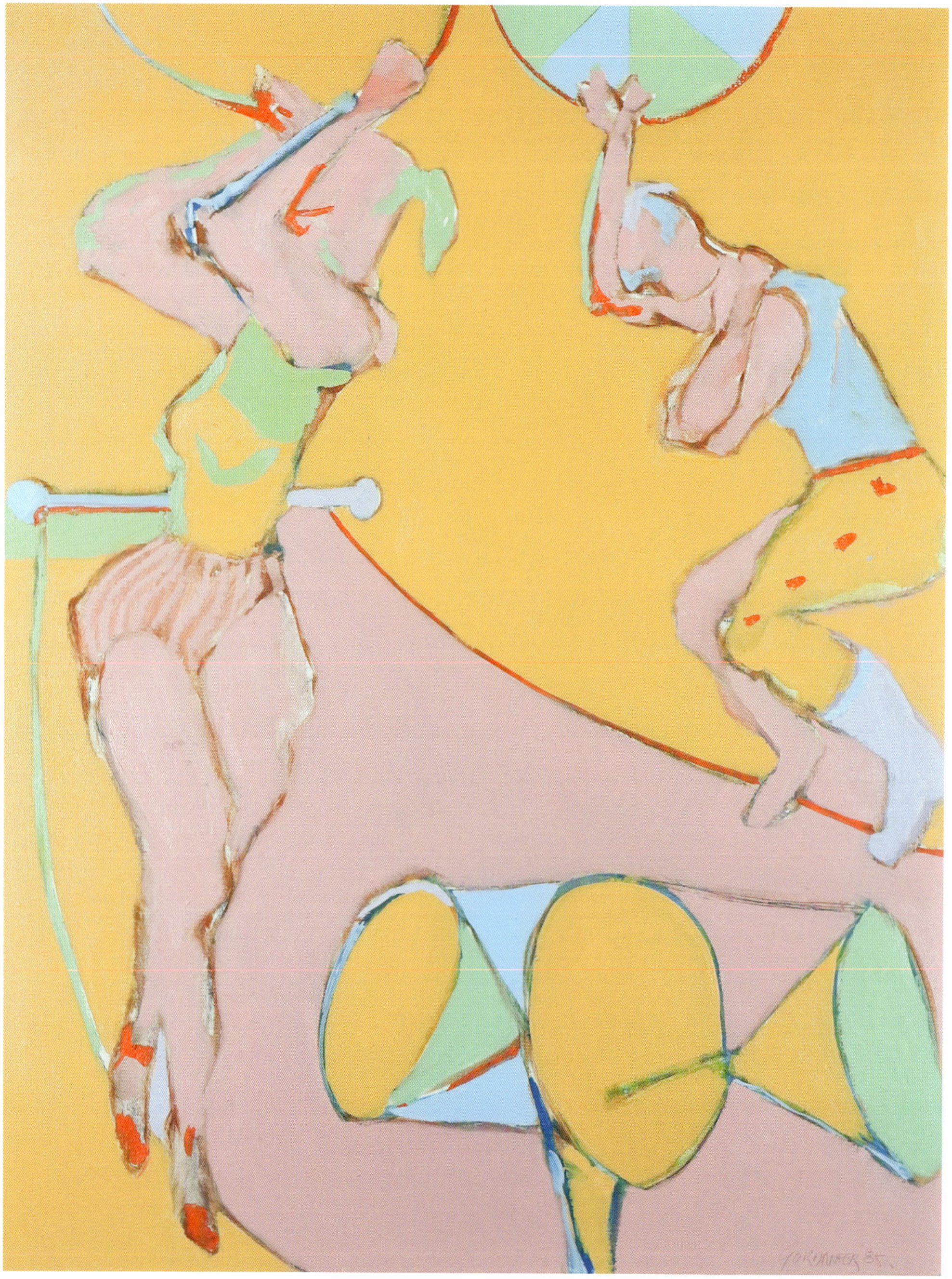

Circus Series: Slack Wire, 1985, oil on canvas

C. Lorens. This group met regularly for almost ten years at Gordaneer's Chapman Street home in Fairfield. The discussions and work revolved around what he and Lorens referred to as the "topological question".[1] Physics, mathematics and spirituality were the starting points for their dialogue. This change in direction gave Gordaneer an opportunity to move past his struggle with modernism and propose a new aesthetic in which the surface of the painting and the application of colour and form were completely renegotiated. Although the group disbanded shortly before Lorens' passing in 1999, Gordaneer feels there continues to be a shared language that arose from the collective experience of the artists in the group, which included his son Jeremy, with whom he has worked all his life, his daughter-in-law Lina Gordaneer and Mark Laver. In the culmination of a decade's worth of probing, Gordaneer exhibited his fifteen-panel diorama *Space Lost, Space Regained* at the University of Victoria's McPherson Library Gallery in 1999.

A turning point for Gordaneer came in 2002 with the exhibition Out of the Shadows at the Fran Willis Gallery. This exhibition marked a relevant and groundbreaking shift in his practice. On a purely formal level, the compositions were heavy with shadows. Psychologically, though, Gordaneer was coming out from under the shadow of the theories that had motivated him over the previous decade. This momentum carries through in his current work. He says he now feels a "licence to be free"[2] and is able to give himself the autonomy he needs to experiment and work through ideas without second-guessing his motives.

According to Lucia Sanroman, who wrote her master's thesis on Gordaneer in 2003, "Gordaneer's painting speaks of stubborn search for autonomy from aesthetic ideologies. It speaks of restless dissension from an expected and encouraged artistic evolution. It speaks of an absolute commitment to painting as a relevant artistic practice despite his marginality. And it articulates all this simply—delighting in the act of making a gesture upon canvas."[3]

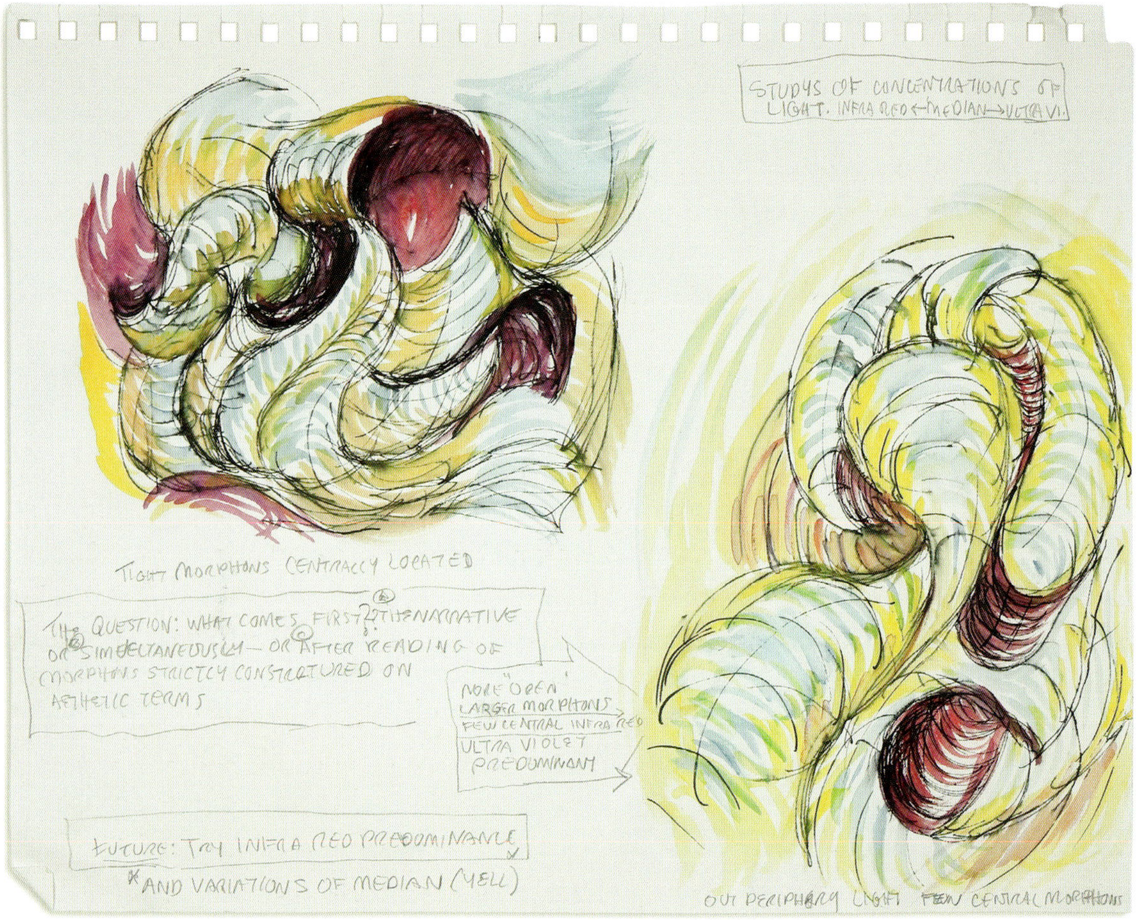

Studies of Concentration of Light, c.1990s, pencil, ink and watercolour on paper

Ideas for Possibilities

> One reaches a state of creation through conscientious work...Preparing to carry it out means nourishing the feeling one has about it with studies that have a sort of similarity to the painting, and then one can make the choice of elements. It is, in fact, these studies that allow the painter to free his unconscious.
>
> Henri Matisse[4]

The copious drawings and sketches that document Gordaneer's environment and artistic evolution are integral to the evolution of his paintings. These studies are a testament to his tenacity for working through theoretical and formal incongruities that surfaced over the decades, as well as to his ongoing preparation before venturing to take paint to canvas. At Doon, he became accustomed to producing a thumbnail sketch of a subject or concept that he was considering for a larger work. While teaching, he also impressed on his students the importance of working through ideas by producing a "rough draft" or visual notes to take to the studio to help inform and bring more resolution to new works.

Every decade of his practice is represented by folders full of experimental drawings, sketches and gouache studies. In some cases there is an obvious correlation to his paintings, which we see in a study for *New York Subway* from 1953. However, the majority of these sketches are ideas for possibilities and only possess a similarity to the painting. The studies Gordaneer produced were never intended as rigorous renderings of their subject matter. Their inherent strength is their immediacy, a sort of visual shorthand. They are an opportunity for the artist to experience uninhibited expression of gesture, composition and colour. The spontaneity that is accessible while in this mode allows for chance, moments of happenstance that bring forth layers of reference points from which to draw. This rigorous practice of drawing set the groundwork for Gordaneer to access uninhibited spaces for creation. Through sketches and studies he became intimately familiar with the physical gestures required to make marks on canvas come together cohesively.

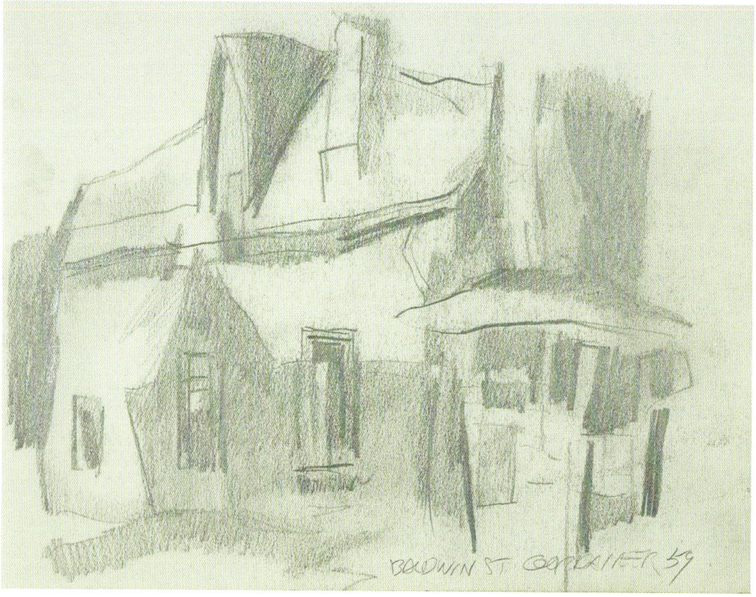

Baldwin St., 1959,
pencil on paper

OPPOSITE PAGE:
Roller Derby, 1971
pen and watercolour
on paper

The subjects in these studies are at times curious and unassuming. Scenes of roller derbies, wrestlers or generic inanimate objects such as furniture and tools seem inconsistent with the complex structures of his paintings. The purpose of the studies was to provide a means for Gordaneer to understand the physical world. His relentless investigation created a natural place where he could subvert these forms into abstraction. Through the years, he continually returned to formal representation to find new gestures for abstraction. An excellent example of the duality in his work is seen in two of his earliest studies, from 1959, of Baldwin Street in Toronto. One drawing is rendered in complete abstraction; the other is a traditional representation of a street scene. His curiosity provoked these enquiries and, as a result, he was able to capture familiar movements and gestures that inadvertently reveal themselves in his compositions.

At times his studies took the shape of a storyboard. Gordaneer would work through several ideas on one page, with notes about the narrative or options for other scenarios of colour. There are examples of this in his drawings from the 1990s, where he probes for ideas through "studies of concentration of light". These drawings included poetic narratives and suggestions on where he could go next. Such "fact-finding missions"[5] also show him drawing source

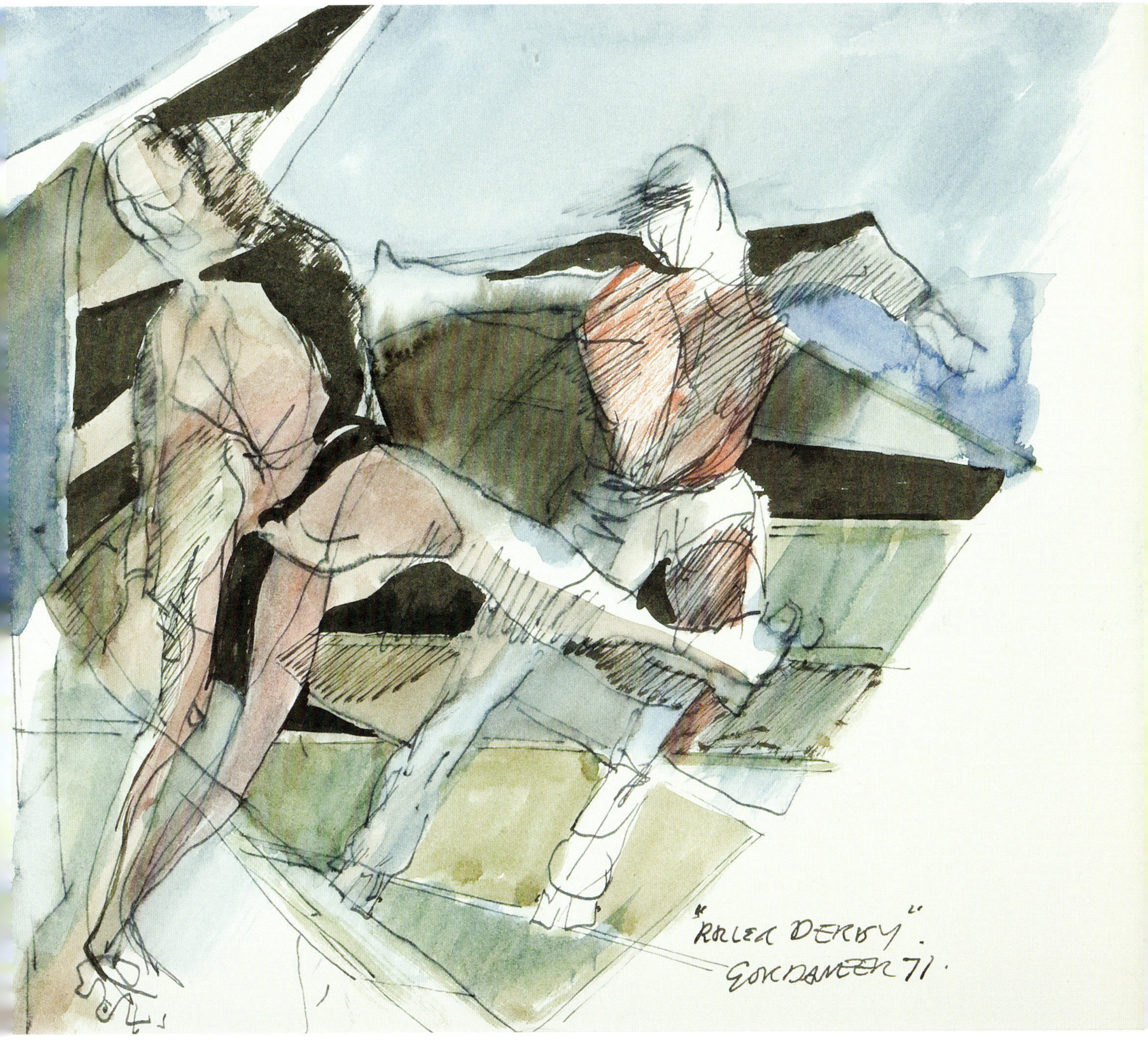
"Roller Derby"

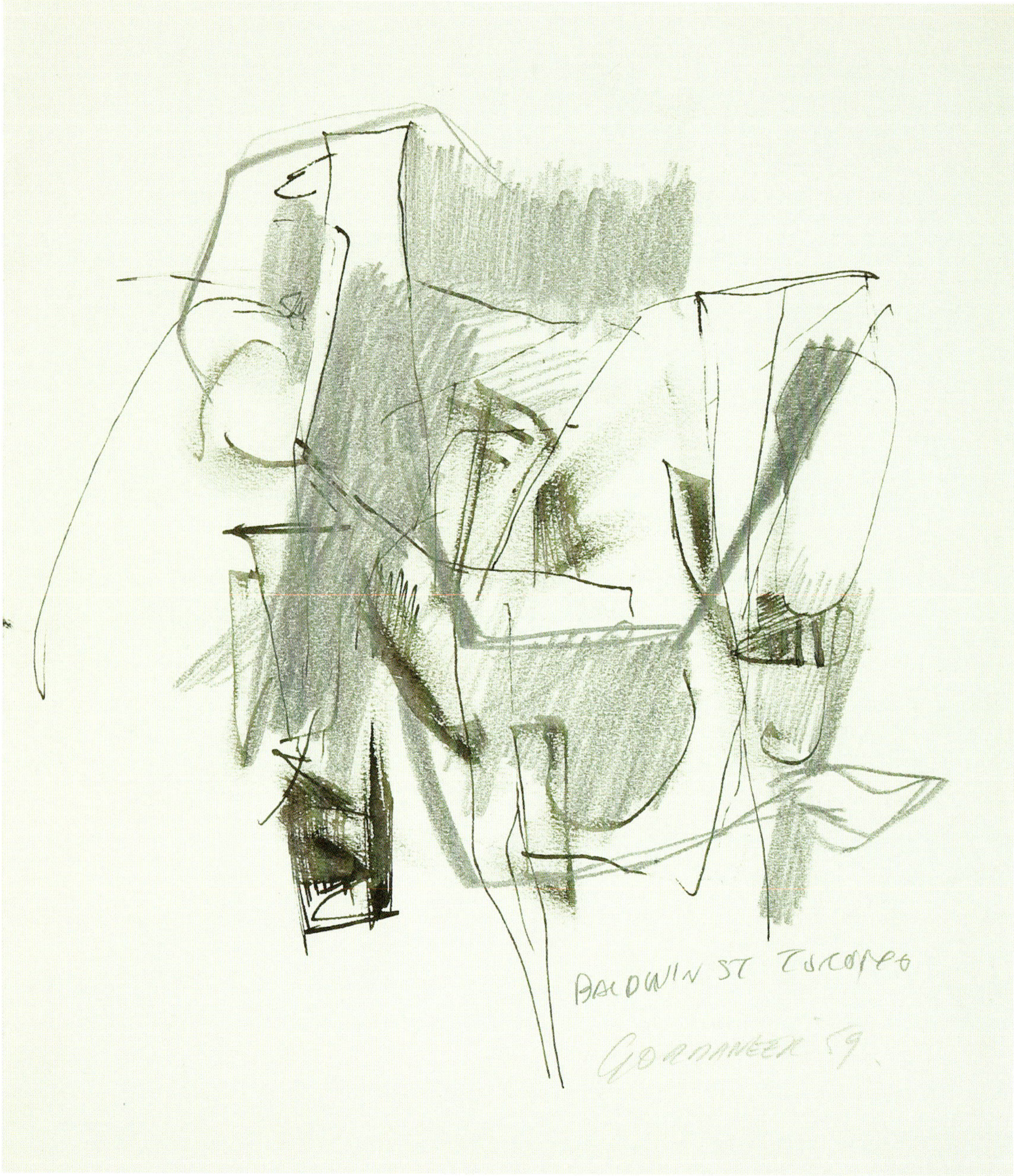

Abstraction of Baldwin St., 1959, pencil on paper

material for his paintings from his immediate surroundings with, for example, a storyboard sketch of an intersection in his Fairfield neighbourhood.

In his most recent body of work, the conflicts and dualities that have been acknowledged in his paintings by curators and critics over the years are now, to a large extent, resolved. He continues to dedicate much of his time to his studio practice, producing new work and seeking out new possibilities. Throughout his career, Gordaneer has chosen to work on his own terms; he feels that he has worked, and continues to work, on the periphery and thus takes his place in "the gaps of the dominant art-historical narrative"[6] in Canadian art history. While his work embodies aspects from the major theories in painting proposed over the last six decades, he has always observed these shifts from a safe distance. This allows him the freedom to move through his career unencumbered. His persistence in his practice stems from his strong work ethic, which drives him to "do something every day"[7]. In this way, Gordaneer continues to keep the creative momentum thriving.

Endnotes

1. Lucia Sanroman, "Embedded Conflict in the Work of James Gordaneer" (Master's thesis, University of Victoria, 2003), p. 114.
2. James Gordaneer, interview with the author, December 10, 2009.
3. Sanroman, "Embedded Conflict," p. 11.
4. Sandra Orienti and Henri Matisse, *Henri Matisse* (London: Hamlyn, 1972), p. 44.
5. Gordaneer, interview.
6. Sanroman, "Embedded Conflict," p. 11.
7. Gordaneer, interview.

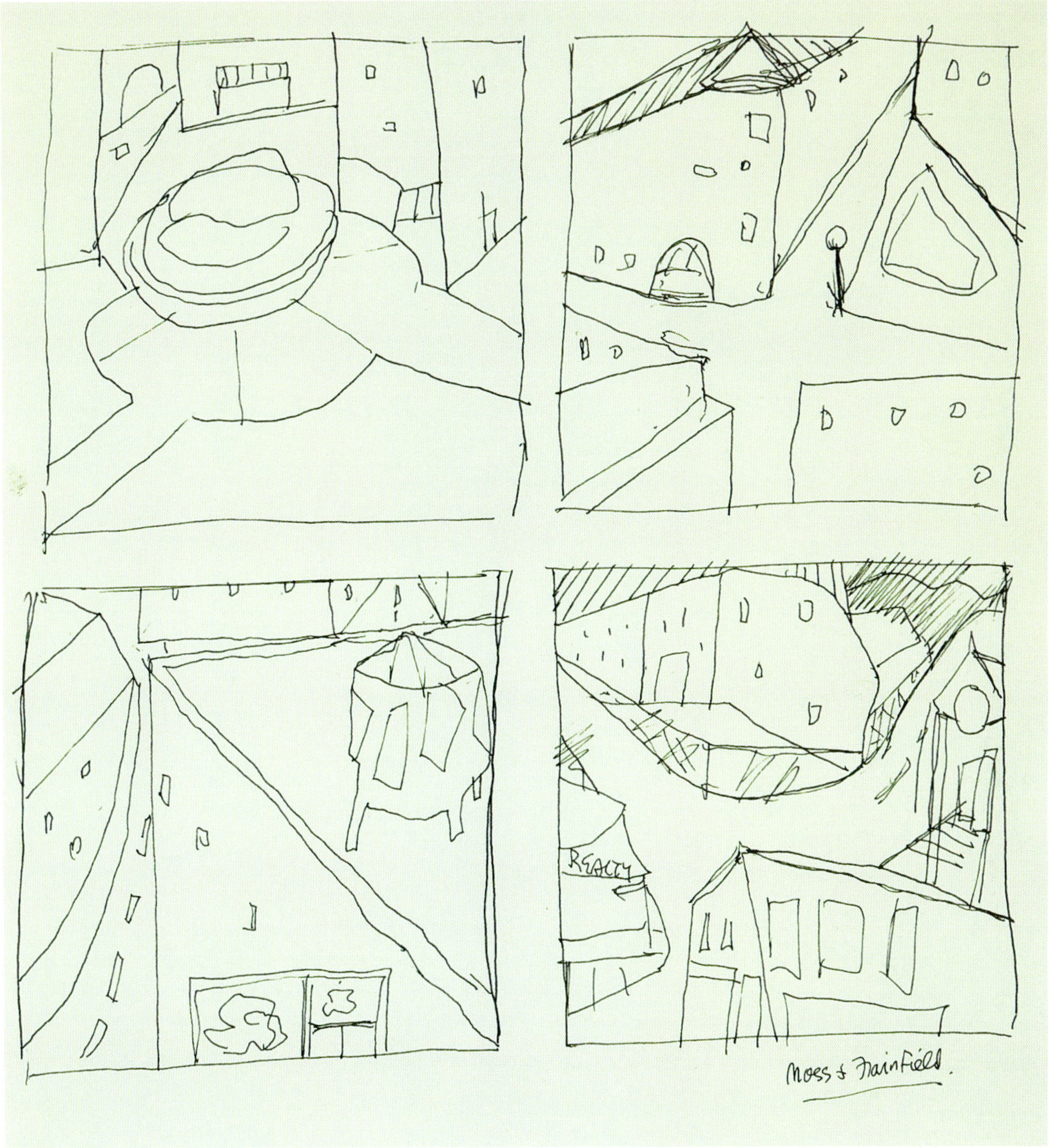

Moss and Fairfield, c.1980s, pen and ink on paper

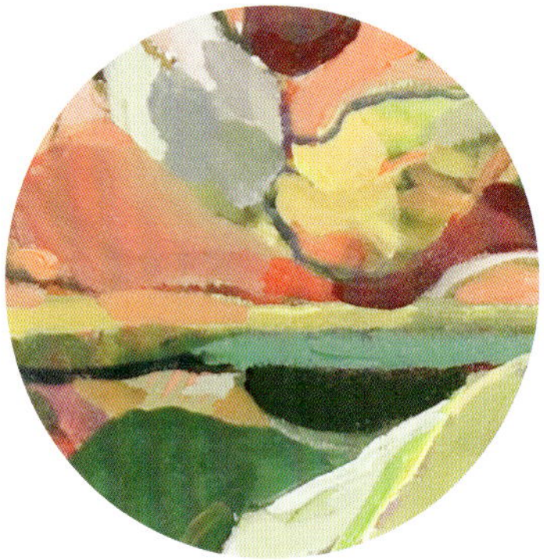

Persistent Longing: Painterly Obsession and the Work of James Gordaneer

LISA BALDISSERA

Painting's imminent and repeated death should be regarded not as a problem, a possibility, or a truth, but as an intermittent accompaniment of painting in the age of modernism. Modernist painting comprises several conceptual elements at partial odds with one another. One part of painting in modernism is the hope of a social contract for art; another is the desire for an immanent critique of representation.

James Elkins

AT THE MUSEU PICASSO IN BARCELONA there is, amongst Pablo Picasso's early works, a modest painting of a barn's interior in darkness. The quiet outline of a wagon, the soft interior barely lit—the scene is painted with the nascent acknowledgement of the changing genre of representation, tinged with postimpressionist concerns of shape and space, yet with a palette of naturalism. Only one note is discordant: a searing light under the barn door unsettles and disrupts this scene. This intrusion slices the painting, tearing the surface of its realism open, seeming to predict the gesture of Lucio Fontana's Concetto Spaziale works, with their refusal of pictorialism, and the conceptual "opening up" of the canvas in the next century to reveal its constructed nature. Picasso achieves this rupture simply: one discordant note in an otherwise seamlessly realistic pictorial surface. Yet this rupture, informed by the modernist impulses emerging in postimpressionism, serves also to introduce the concerns that would preoccupy the discourse on painting throughout the twentieth century—the influence of modernism, which marked debates about painting in the first half of the century, followed by conceptual approaches to painting within the postmodern debates of both artists and critics, which attempted to resolve this discursive schism.

Throughout the century, painting was burdened with a weighty and well-defined linear trajectory, which the critique put forward by modernist painting underscored. In his theories, Clement Greenberg in particular proposed a "devolution, an unraveling" of art historical

From Elkins' essay "Why Nothing Can Be Accomplished in Painting, and Why It Is Important to Keep Trying," *Circa* 109 (Autumn 2004).

tradition that would refuse the romanticism and spatial illusionism of realist representation, which could no longer be tolerated in a postwar consciousness.[1] Greenberg posited an art form that was an evolutionary step beyond the concerns of previous movements, formulating its own methodologies and interacting directly as an object with its audience. In retrospect, this attempt gave rise to certain kinds of proscriptive and reductive definitions, both in Greenberg's model and in the interpretation of some of the practitioners of modern painting as they strove to create a nonobjective art form, freed from representation and, indeed, from any kind of extraneous projection outside its own terms of objecthood. Looking back, we can see how the philosophical pressures of such a movement challenged many painters and critics. In fact, as American art critic James Elkins asserts, "The decision about the importance and relevance of history is the most fundamental one in writing about painting even now, long after modernism's particular sense of painting's history has dissolved and dispersed."[2]

Painting in the twenty-first century is well served by an alternative model put forward by Gilles Deleuze and Félix Guattari in their discussions of aesthetic innovation and development. In their essay "A Thousand Plateaus," the philosophers employ a model based on the idea of a rhizome, an entity that grows ganglion-like, its "nerve" centre distributed throughout each of its extensions and therefore decentred, destabilized and ever transferring knowledge/nutrients from one site to another. In his book *Art Encounters Deleuze and Guattari: Thought Beyond Representation*, Simon O'Sullivan describes it this way:

> A rhizome is a system, or anti-system, without centre or indeed any central organising motif. It is a flat system in which the individual nodal points can be, and are, connected to one another in a non-hierarchical manner. A rhizome then fosters transversal connections and communications between heterogeneous locations and events. Indeed a rhizome, ultimately, is composed not of points but of the lines between these points. The rhizome is a paradigmatic example of the invention of a concept. In its expanded sense it might also be understood as the presentation of a new "image of thought" inasmuch as it allows us to think thought differently, in this case to think

> differently and in opposition to root-like, or tree-like, structures, which, as Deleuze and Guattari demonstrate in this first plateau, are ubiquitous within Western thought and culture.[3]

The rhizome may best characterize painting's current state and could also be posited as its "expressionist" characteristic: rather than revealing the artist's subjectivity, this is the expression of painting itself, the reflexive and conversational quality of its ongoing experiment. This is epitomized in the new work of young Canadian artists such as Etienne Zack, Wil Murray, Amanda Reeves and Ryan Sluggett. One can roam the surface of their paintings and spot the aesthetic, conceptual and stylistic borrowings, which are present in a spatially ahistorical and atemporal order—similar to sociograms, the flat system of the world wide web: an "idea cluster," which also occupies the abstract surface of the canvas. In this way, the idea of representation is usurped, the canvas becoming instead a fluid and elegant semiotic consideration of painting's history. Elkins writes:

> This is the lesson that seems so difficult for the art world: despite the fundamental critique launched by minimalism, despite the rise of so many new media, despite the many rumors of its death, despite everything, painting remains the central medium for the articulation and historiography of the visual arts...painting is crucial for the conceptualization of visual art, and to art's sense of its own history.[4]

Modernity persists as an unfinished project, alongside the postmodern, and so do its pre-rhizomatic roots in the practice of painting. It is useful, then, to think of its contemporary manifestation as a kind of post abstraction functioning within postmodernism. In the same way post minimalism functioned in relation to its precursor, minimalism, post abstraction acknowledges the aesthetic and ideological influences that both historically and contemporaneously inform the work. Unable to sustain ideals of purity, as high modernism demanded, post abstraction takes place fully in the flow of subjectivities—not of the individual, necessarily, but subjectivities intrinsic to painting's history, a rhizomatic infection of any formal expression.

Within the Canadian tradition, the landscape had become an armature for the exploration of a modernist practice. Artists employed the specificity of the landscape to translate the concerns of European modernity into terms that made sense within the burgeoning industrial and social context of their own post-imperialist moment. Modernity in Canada, therefore, had a specific task: to create an aesthetic movement which acknowledged a sophisticated cultural presence in Canada and which could be used in service to the emerging notion of Canadian identity as distinct from empire, whether British or American. Understandably, the modernism of European and American postwar painting required a fresh interpretation. It was this milieu Gordaneer entered with his early work.

Since the 1940s, James Gordaneer has made a daily practice of painting. Prolific, energetic, and possessing the skill of an artist who has explored the aesthetic frontiers of his generation, he has investigated the material, conceptual and philosophical territories for six decades, riding the currents of twentieth-century debates about painting's place in contemporary art.

As a young painter in southern Ontario, Gordaneer trained at the Doon School of Fine Art in the early 1950s. A summer program that required no entrance portfolio, this was a viable option for young painters who wished to refuse the academy—an act that was not regarded as a liability, as art schools in Canada were still in their infancy, and identification as an "amateur" carried with it the status of innovator, freed from aesthetic convention and old-school rules. At Doon, Gordaneer studied with the best modernist painters of the post-Group of Seven generation; Jock Macdonald, Carl Schaefer, Jack Bechtel, Alex Millar and, before Gordaneer's time, Frederick Varley had been instrumental in the school's development. It was here that Gordaneer began to work directly in the landscape and developed his lifelong practice of working *en plein air*. Using nature as a resource—not as muse but as a framework on which to hang his aesthetic and philosophical questions about art making—Gordaneer endeavoured to articulate the concerns that guided him through painting's most contested century.

Inheriting the early modernity of the Group of Seven and the Ashcan painters, Gordaneer worked diverse subjects: landscape, figure, cityscape and still life (for example, see the works

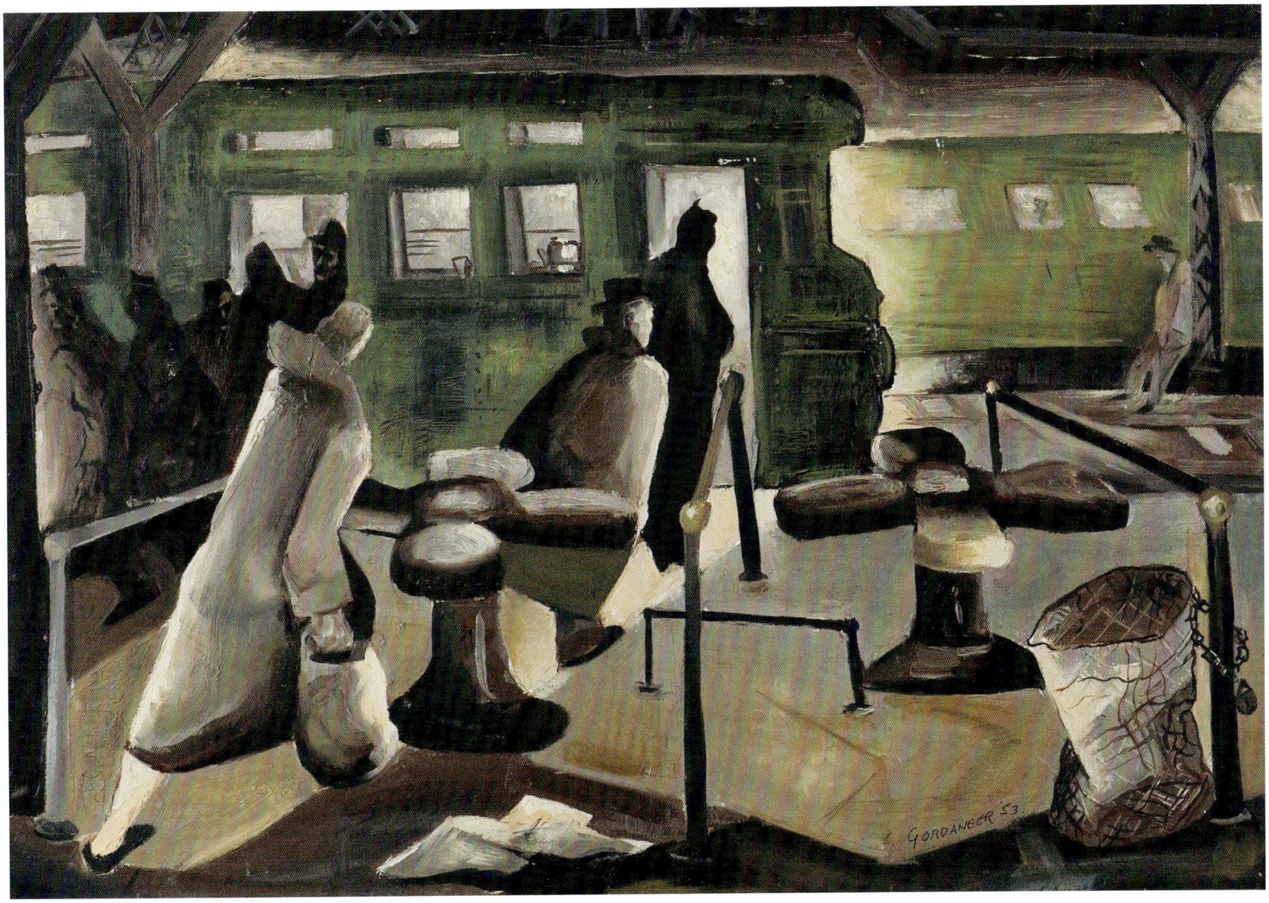

New York Subway, 1953, oil on masonite

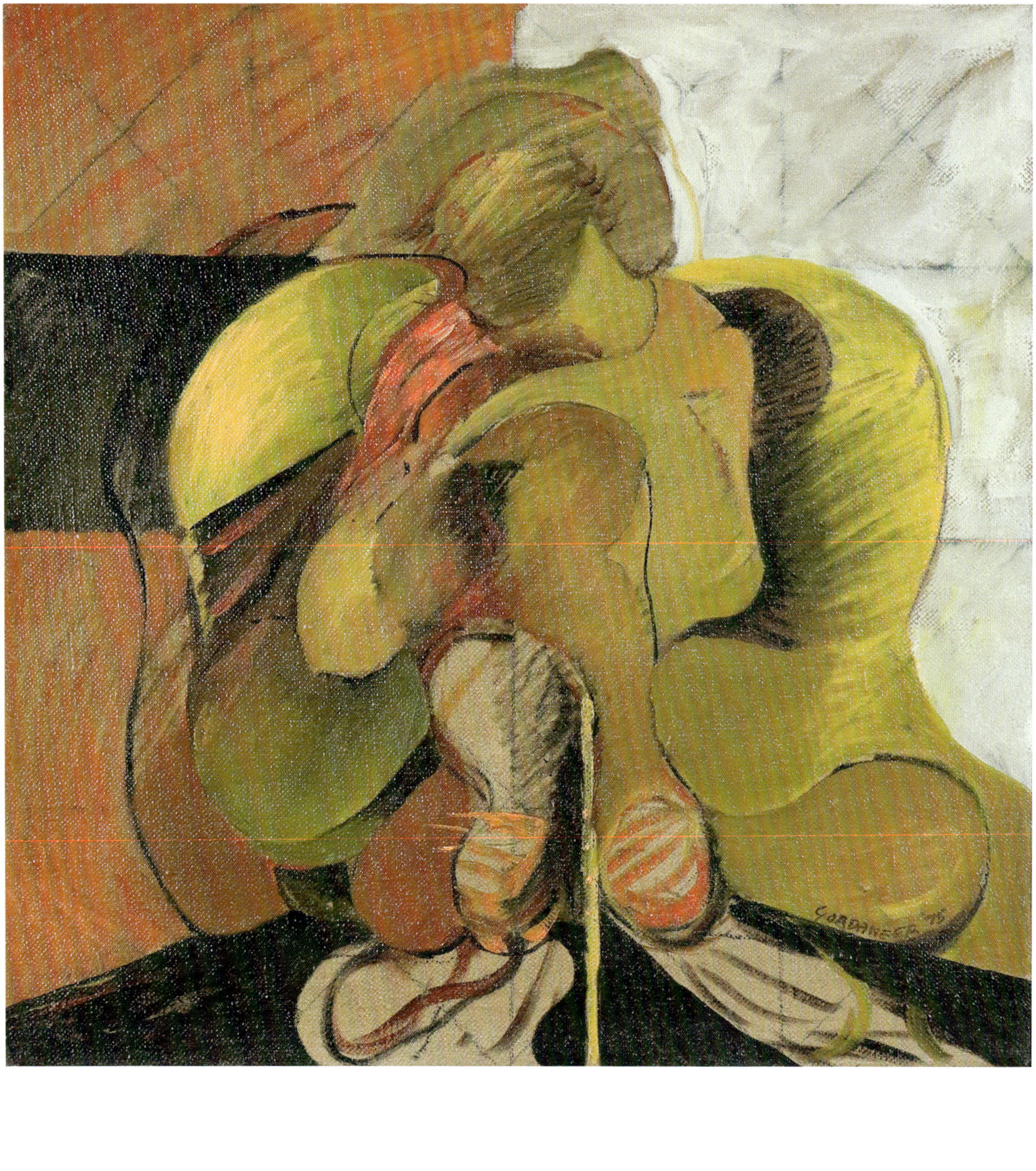

Enigma, 1976, oil on linen

New York Subway and *Orrie's Place, Whitney ON*). His earliest works are marked by a confident compositional and spatial sense, in which the painter's vision overtakes the naturalism of the scene. This led to further experimentation with form. Beginning in 1956, after his first trip to San Miguel de Allende, Gordaneer's work exhibited the influence of Mexican modernism. After visiting an exhibition at the Art Gallery of Ontario (AGO), Gordaneer was inspired by the examples of Spanish modernism that he had seen there, including works adopting Picasso's great modern contribution, cubism (see Gordaneer's *Clown* and *Circus-Between Acts*).

Canadian painters at that time were influenced by this European modernism, as well as by the more austere version that was brewing in America. In Europe, modernity retained an expressive quality—surface, composition, colour were still eccentric and subjective territories, as was the occasional figurative reference in these works, which revealed the artists' decisions at every juncture, every ridge, every chromatic transition. Distinct from their American peers, the modern work of Arshile Gorky and Hans Hoffmann, through his New York School in America, was also an influence on Gordaneer in those early days, as were Harold Town, whose work he had seen at the AGO, and the Automatistes of Quebec, including the loose painterly abstraction of Paul Emile Borduas.

After trips to Ibiza and Paris, where he encountered abstract expressionism first-hand, Gordaneer earned attention in Toronto for his works of lyrical abstraction. Examples such as *Autumn Growth* and *Red Abstraction* reveal a painter of great gifts and confidence. Unfortunately, there are no pieces from this stylistic period in the exhibition; in many cases the works locations are unknown, other then *Autumn Growth* which is in the collection of the Robert McLaughlin Gallery in Ontario.

Gordaneer continued this exploration of nonobjective painting through the early 1960s as he processed these influences. Expressive abstract forms, often obliquely referencing landscape or derived from nature, make their way into the work and continued to do so into the later part of the decade. Gordaneer's work from the late 60s and early 70s has been mistakenly associated with the surrealist movement (see, for example, *Space Station*, *Enigma*, *Pineapples and Eggplant*), but in my view this is only because its automatiste and collage origins stylistically suggest this association; his philosophical intent is quite distinct from surrealism's manifestos.

Rather, Gordaneer's work throughout his career clearly and consistently exhibits links to the aesthetic expressionism I have described earlier in this essay—not that of the artist's own subjectivity, but of an investigation that explores the conditions for making paintings, in which brushwork, surface, graphic form and drawing continue to take their place in the realization of the work in conceptual and historical terms.

For many painters of his generation, the struggle to find a distinct style, if abstract expressionism and post-painterly abstraction (particularly in mid and late century) were not intuitive approaches, became a lifelong identity crisis. This predicament can be seen in the careers of other painters in Canada—including Patterson Ewan and the post-1960s work of the Regina Five (Donald Jarvis, Doug Morton, Ted Godwin, Ron Bloore, Ron MacKay and Ken Lochhead)—and the United States—including Milton Avery, Larry Rivers, Helen Frankenthaler and Philip Guston. Gordaneer particularly admired Guston's writings, which provided encouragement. He marked the following passage by Guston:

> There is something ridiculous and miserly in the myth we inherit from abstract art: That painting is autonomous, pure and for itself, therefore we habitually analyze its ingredients and define its limits. Painting is "impure." It is the adjustments of "impurities" which force its continuity. We are image makers and image ridden.[5]

Gordaneer began to articulate his unease with the proscriptive nature of modernist abstraction and to develop his own rationale for works that moved into decisively new critical territory.

In the later 1970s, Gordaneer started to incorporate the expressive qualities of the early part of the decade into his work, returning again to the representation that had occupied him in the early part of his career. Work from this period opens up into a pictorialism that integrates the abstraction of the 1950s and 60s (see *Palaeo Plain*, for example). A few years later, after moving to Victoria, Gordaneer developed a close relationship with Jack Wise, whose use of the calligraphic mark emerged in Gordaneer's own brushwork. He set to work developing a new approach to subject matter that was mediated by the aesthetic developments of his first

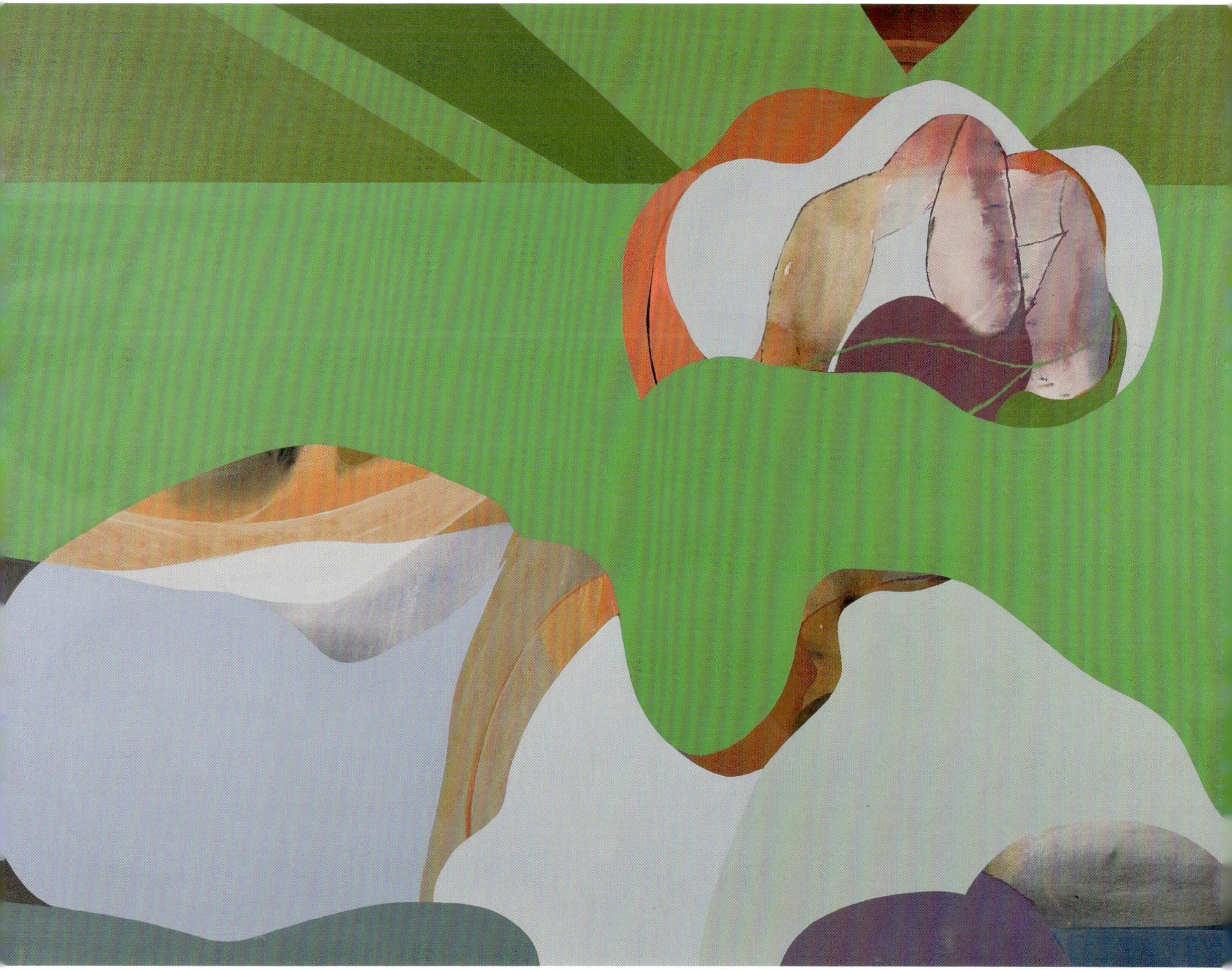

Palaeo Plain, 1970 , acrylic on canvas

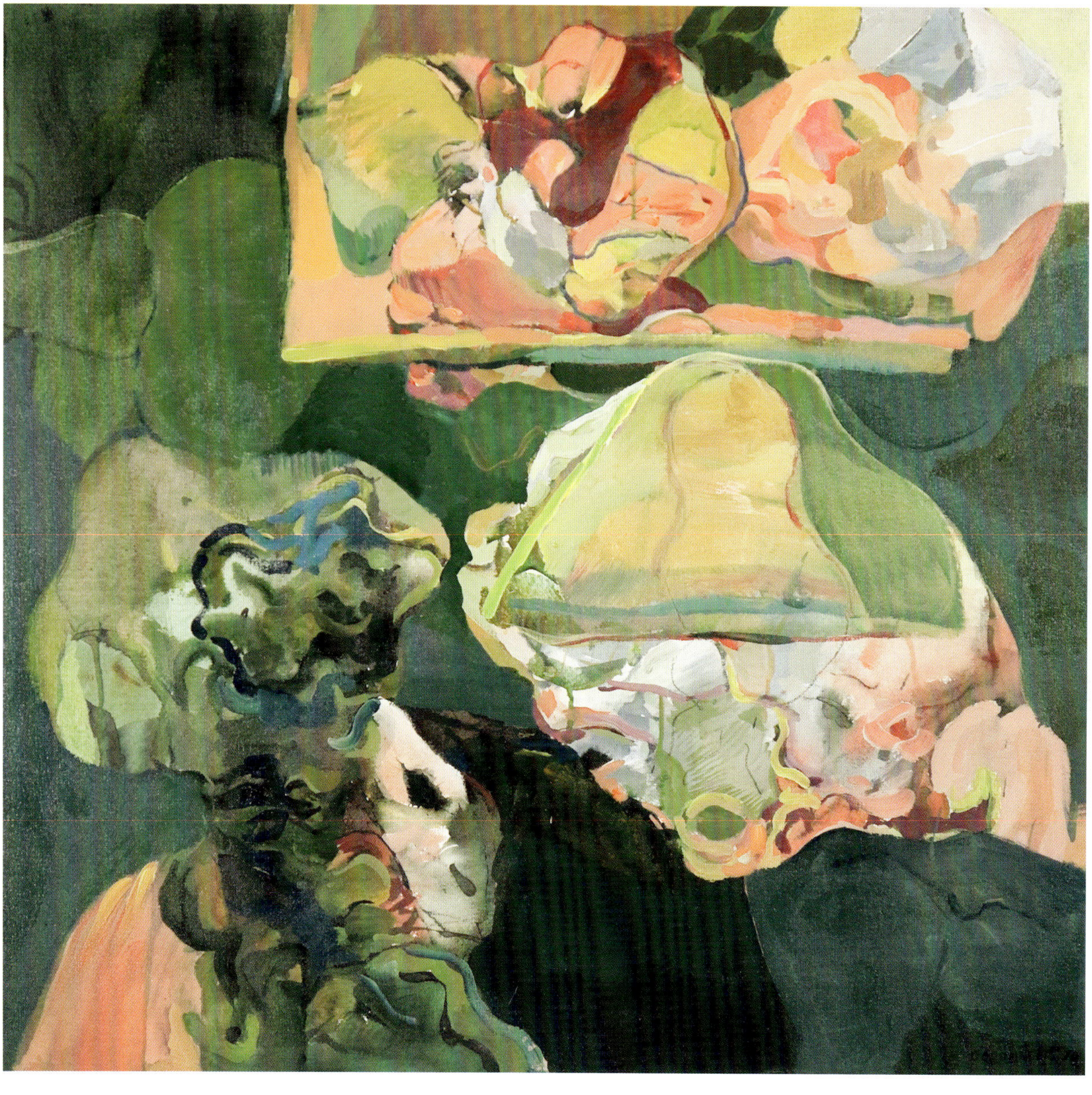

Atrium in Hades, 1976, oil on linen

twenty-five years, synthesized into an ambitious assertion of his own preoccupations, outside the project of modernism that occupied many Toronto-based artists at that time.

It seemed fortuitous that the move to Victoria allowed Gordaneer to encounter a new landscape and new influences, such as Wise. At the same time, many other painters in Canada were seeking alternatives and likewise injecting more subjective concerns into their work with realism, figuration and other quasi-representational methods. In the east were Alex Colville and his peers; in central Canada, Patterson Ewan and Ivan Eyre. At this time, early postmodernism, with its focus on subjectivity, was offering a strenuous critique of modernism, albeit not strictly within the territory of painting, but in new media, sculpture, installation and other conceptual practices. As much as modernity was ripe for problematization, however, it was still difficult to wrestle painting back from its imperatives.

Despite this, the late 70s marked a period of great productivity and freedom for Gordaneer, who felt collegial support in Victoria as well as a growing confidence in his own resistance to Greenbergian modernism. Works such as *Atrium in Hades* and *Arbutus Cove* reveal his reenergized vision. Gordaneer joined the Victoria College of Art and was involved briefly in its "experimental year" in 1981, when all instructors and students were charged with working only in the style of hard edge abstraction. Ideals of the sublime and modernist purity returned to haunt Gordaneer in what must have felt like déjà vu, and he was once again challenged to articulate his ideas. But Gordaneer, ever the innovator and survivor, took what he felt was best from this experience; work following 1981 shows the flat areas of colour and reduced spatial qualities that were a legacy of this period. *Band Stand* (from the *Beacon Hill Park Series*) and *Slack Wire* (from the *Circus Series*) are emblematic of this new vision. The resulting series met with critical success locally.

Still, Gordaneer felt a need to articulate finally his position in relation to modernity, and in this endeavour he found a partner, Raymond Lorens. During the 1990s, his conversations with Lorens, a theologian and philosopher, resulted in a kind of collaborative approach to painting influenced by the emerging studies of quantum physics and topological mathematics.[6] Works such as *Licence*, produced during this period, were an attempt to illustrate the provisional and relational nature of the new physics. They demonstrate a responsiveness and multivalence that seemed perfectly suited to articulating the equally destabilizing and decentralized ideas of postmodernism. Working together assiduously from 1992 to 1999, the two men attempted to define a philosophy that could articulate what they saw as the failures of modernism and the omissions of postmodernism. The Chapman Group, formed around these theories, included other artists in Victoria and worked cohesively for almost a decade, disbanding finally in 1999, followed, sadly, by the sudden death of Lorens in the same year.

In the decade since then, Gordaneer's career, as always, has been marked by prodigious output. Having synthesized the model he developed with Lorens, Gordaneer began to resituate himself. An artist like Gordaneer, who witnessed first-hand the major developments of twentieth-century painting as they emerged, was implicated in that history's ideological weight and directive. Arriving on his own at the rhizomatic approach posited by Deleuze and Guattari, Gordaneer emerges both as witness and as senior painter. Reflecting once again on the movements and innovations that define his career, Gordaneer has, in his newest works, come to terms with painting's history—his own progression through it, as well as the major forces which marked the century. The work is forceful, an aesthetic meteor approaching the Earth, which brings with it all the particles of its journey across time and galaxies. Gordaneer's references are not simply art historical quotes, a listing of categorical signifiers to mark the fractured nature of current painting debate, but a *catalogue raisonné*—comprised not of the artist's individual works, but of sixty years of conceptual and formal interrogations, fully and finally synthesized.

Endnotes

1. Clement Greenberg, "Modernist Painting," in *Forum Lectures* (Washington, DC: Voice of America, 1960). Available online at http://www.sharecom.ca/greenberg/modernism.html

2. James Elkins, "Why Nothing Can Be Accomplished in Painting, and Why It Is Important to Keep Trying," *Circa* 109 (Autumn 2004), pp. 38–41.

3. Simon O' Sullivan, *Art Encounters Deleuze and Guattari: Thought beyond Representation* (London: Palgrave Macmillan, 2006), pp. 12–13.

4. James Elkins, "Why Nothing Can Be Accomplished."

5. Lucia Sanroman notes Gordaneer's marking of the passage in her thesis on Gordaneer: "Embedded Conflict in the Work of James Gordaneer" (Master's thesis, University of Victoria, 2003), p. 109. The passage is from Robert Storr, *Philip Guston* (New York: Abbeville Press, 1986), p. 34.

6. Sanroman, "Embedded Conflict," p. 114.

Works of Art

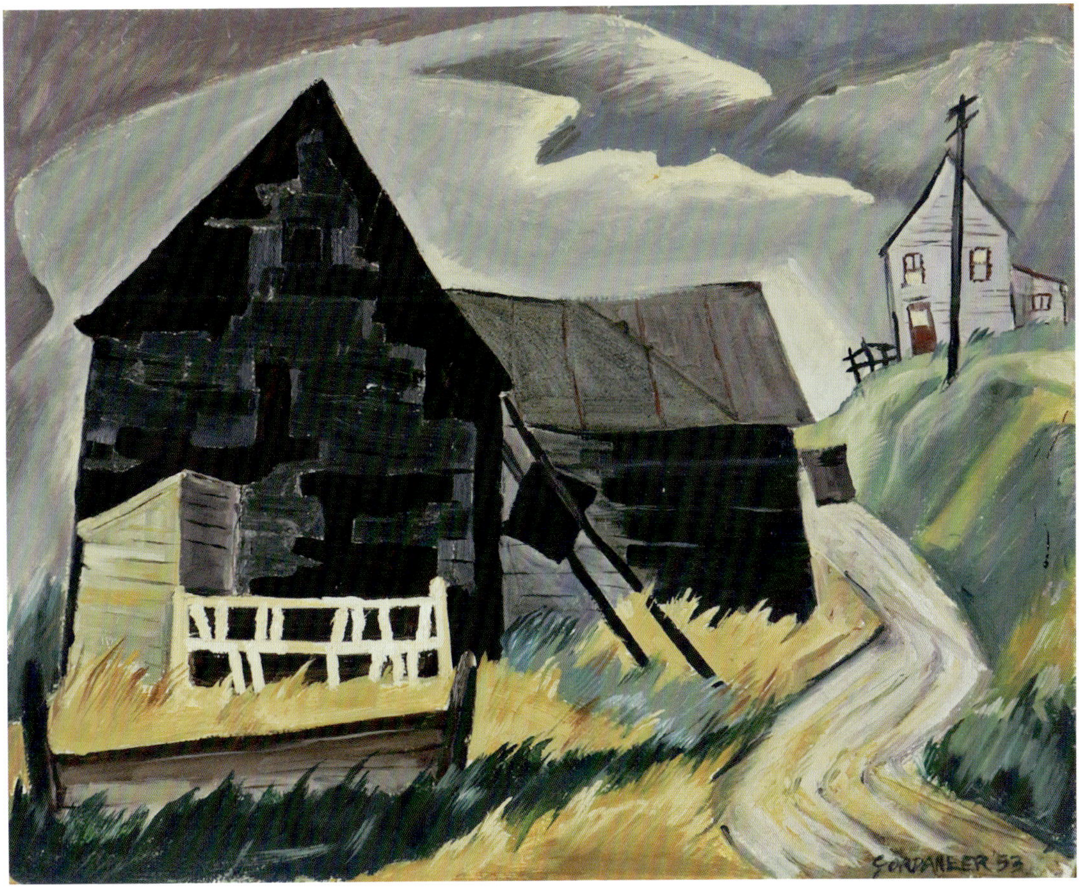

Barns, Whitney ON, 1953, oil on masonite

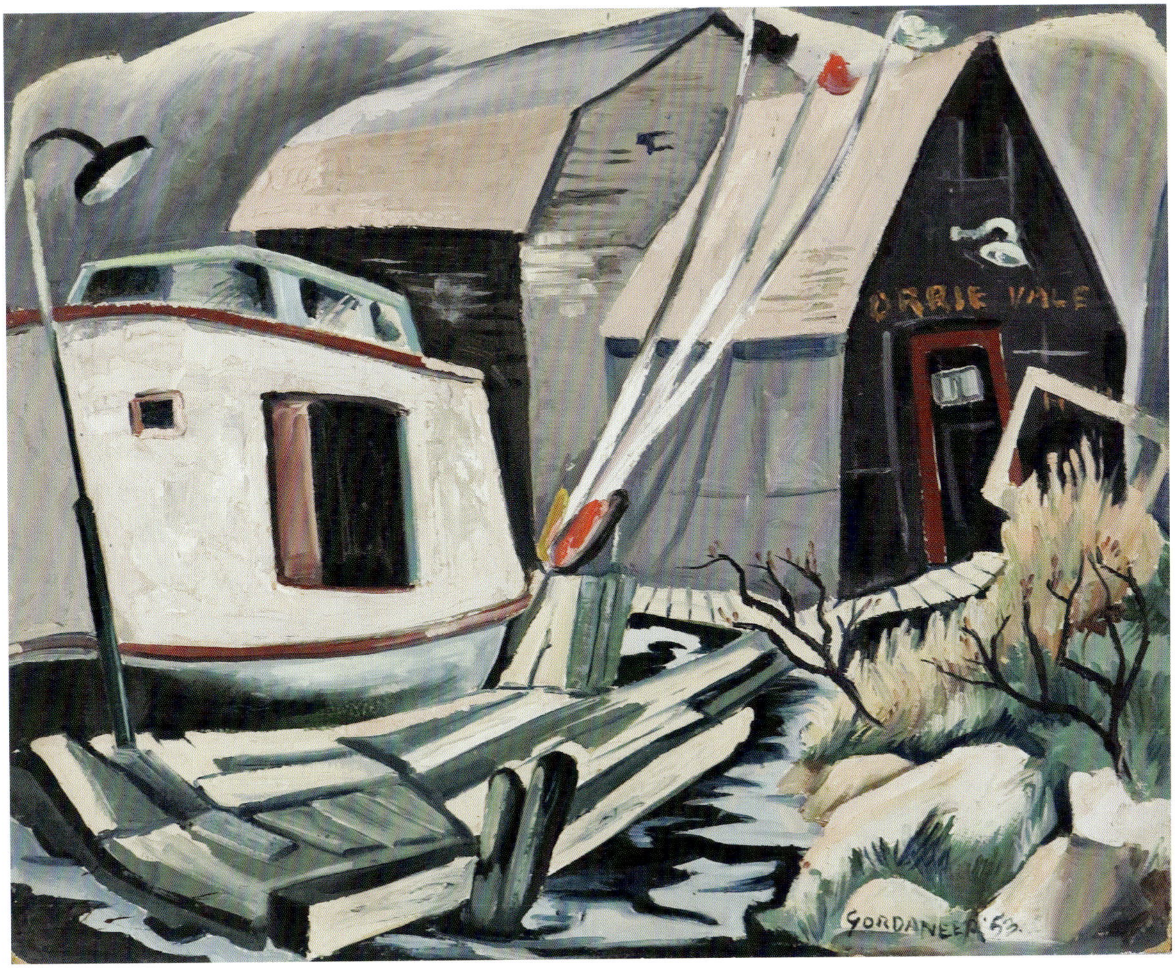

Orrie's Place, Whitney ON, 1953, oil on masonite

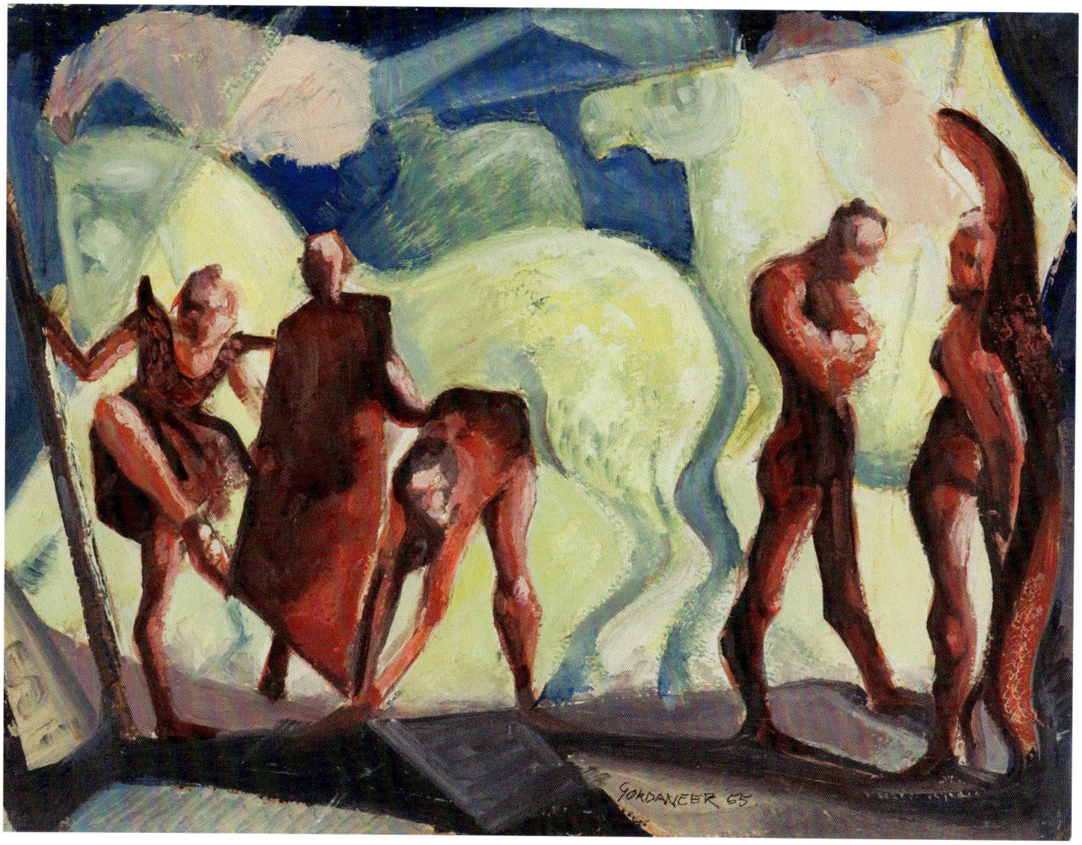

Circus — Between Acts, 1954, oil on masonite

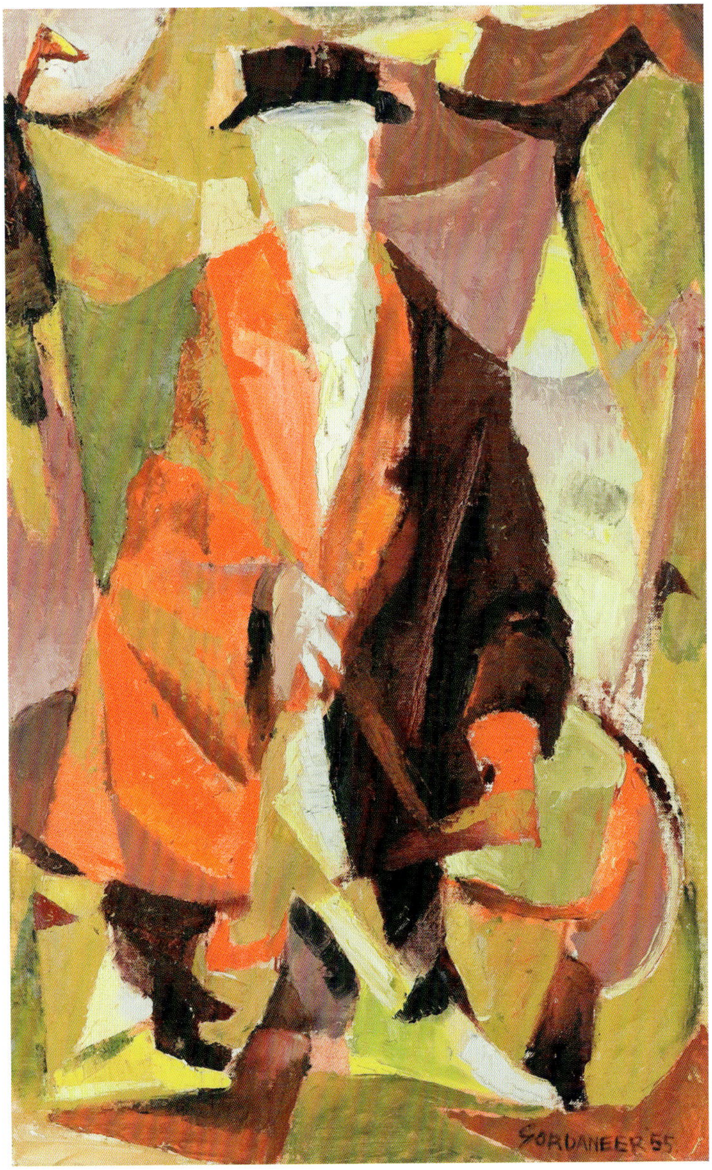

Clown, 1955, oil on masonite

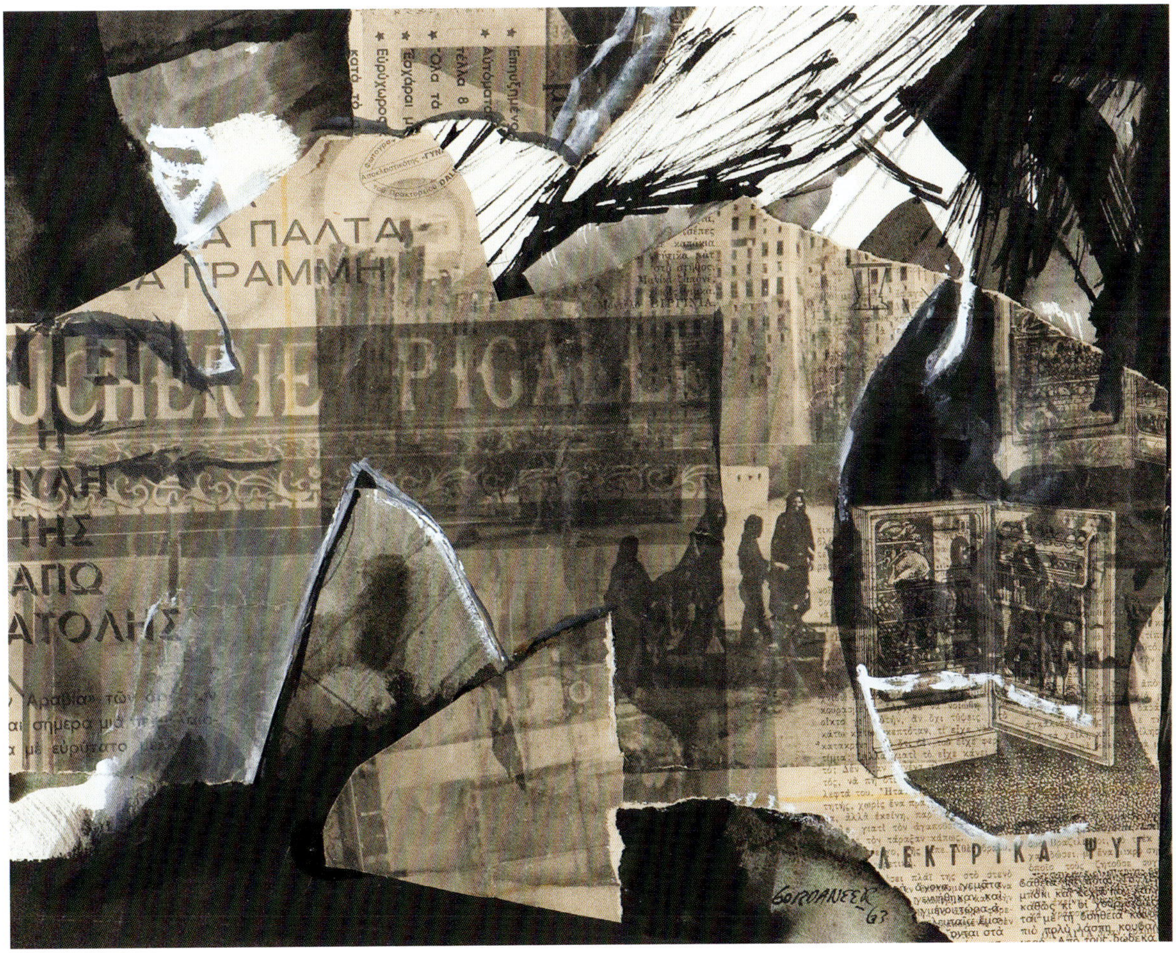

Greek Collage, 1963, newsprint, glue and ink on paper

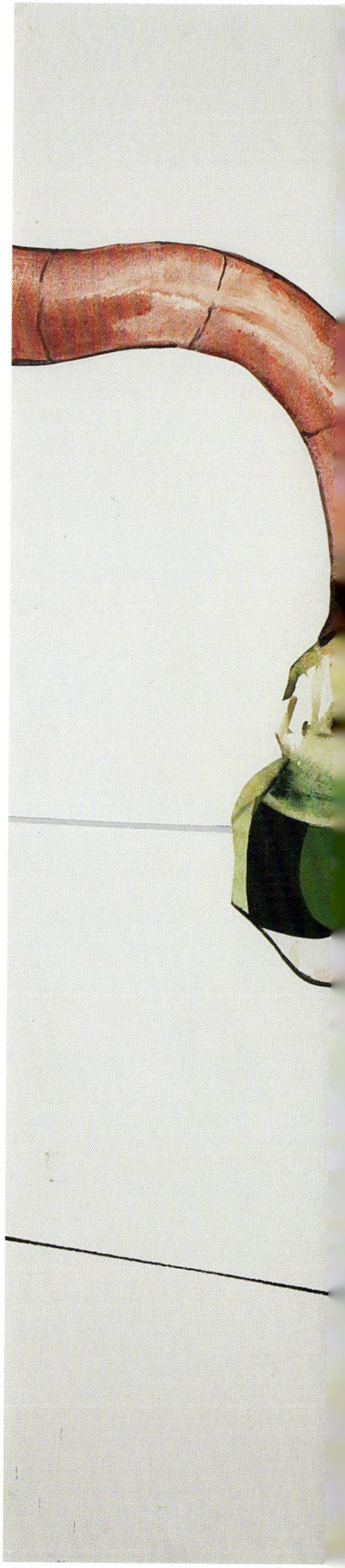

Space Station, 1969, acrylic on canvas

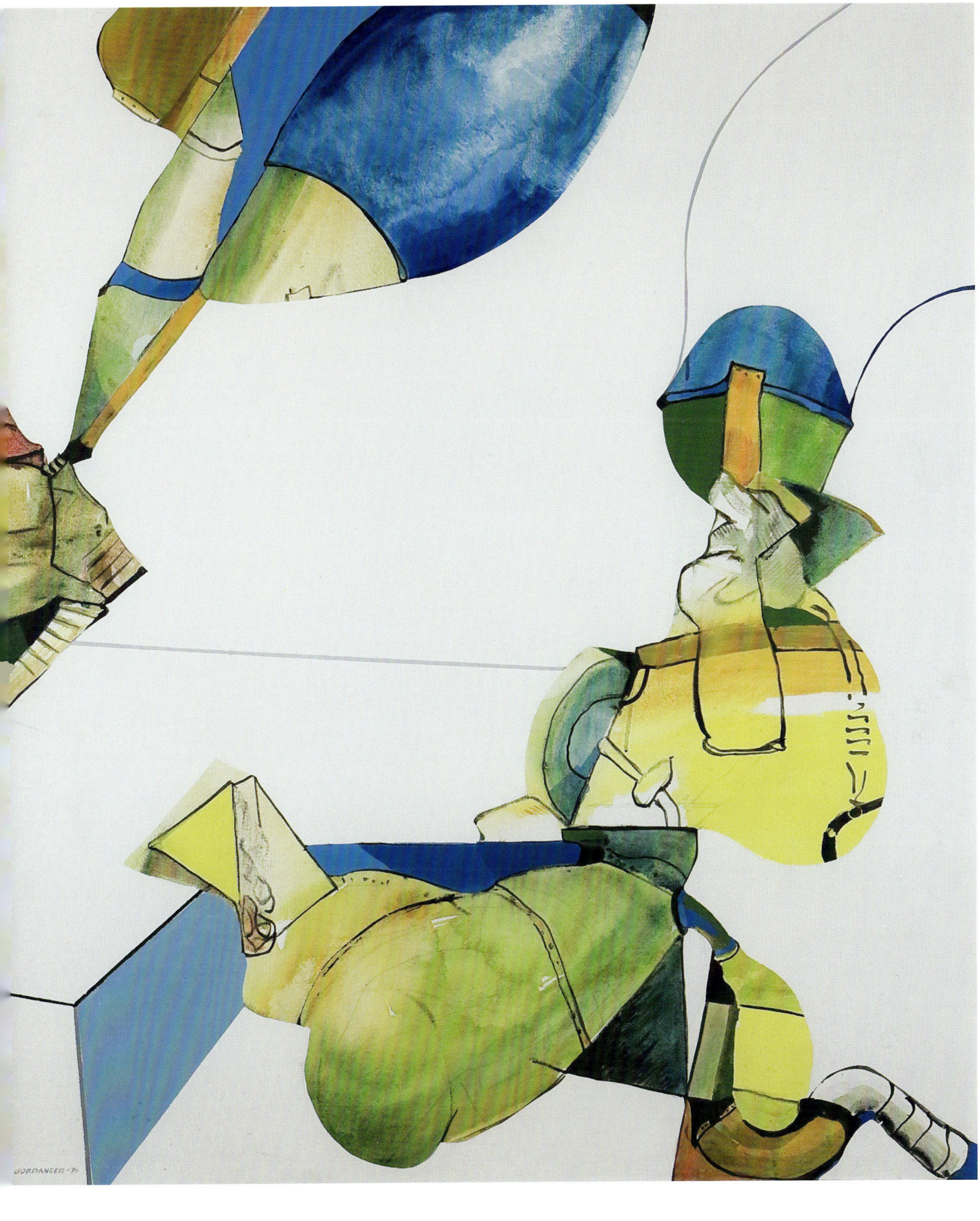
GORDANEER '70

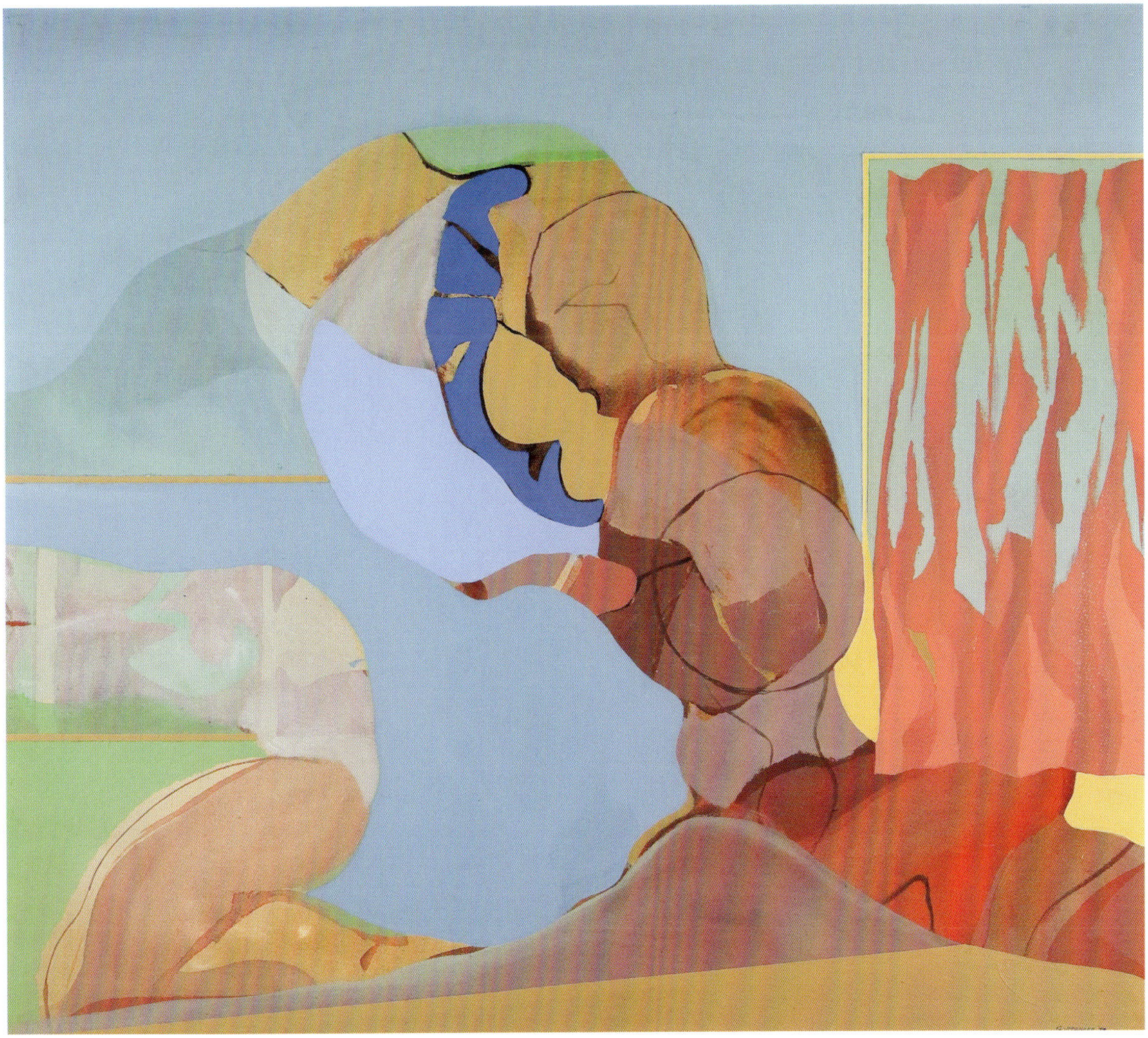

Spring Occurrence, 1973, oil on canvas

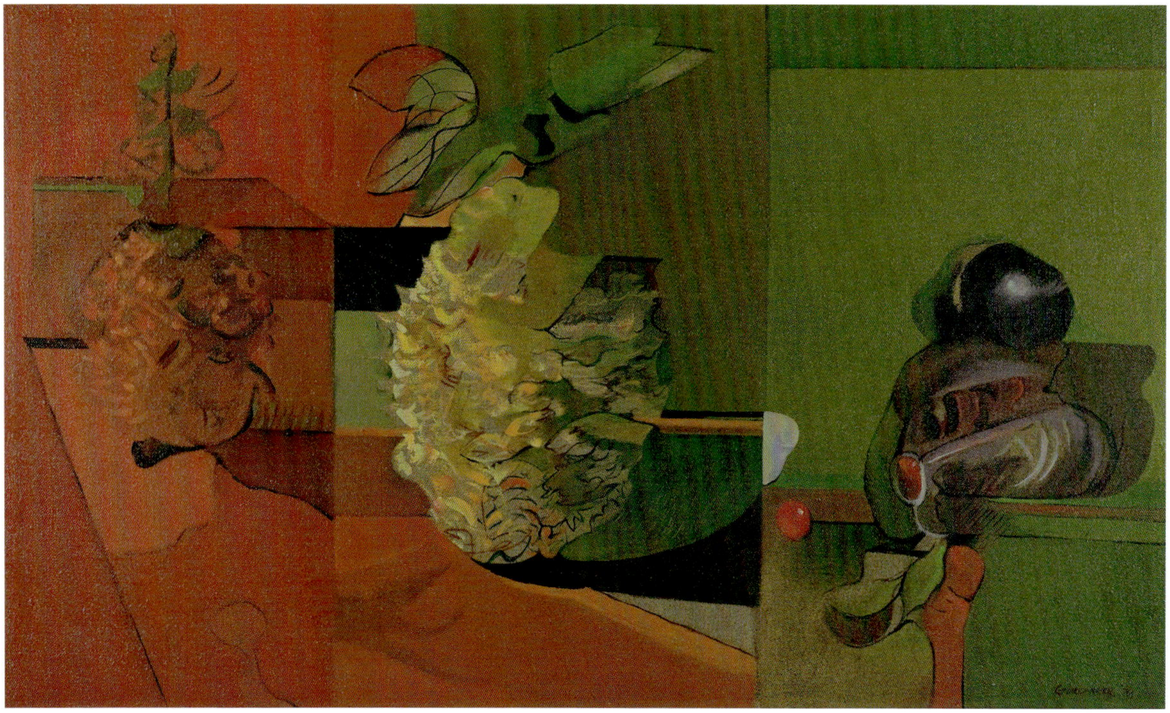

Pineapples and Eggplant, 1974, oil on linen

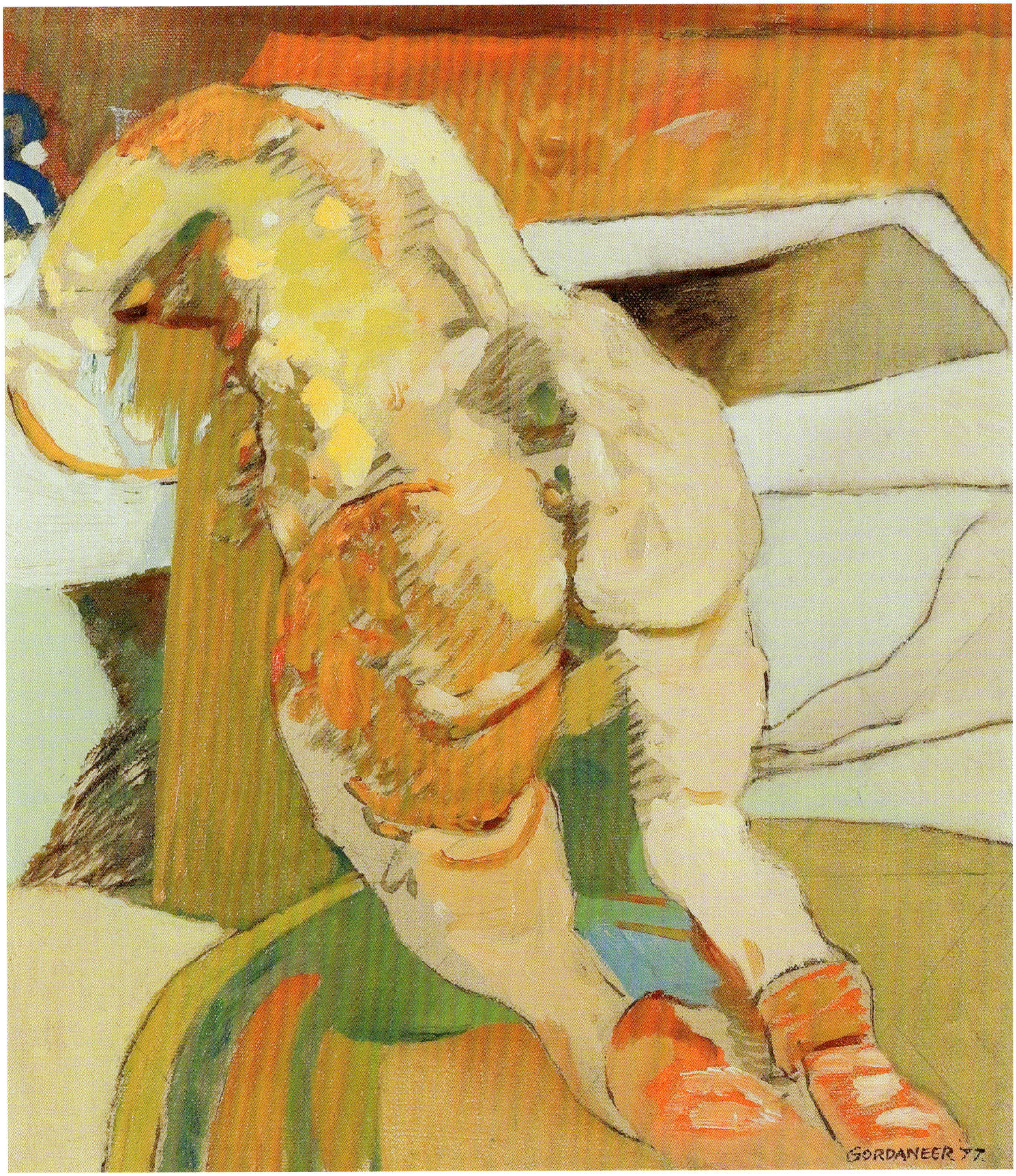

Washing Her Hair, 1977, oil on canvas

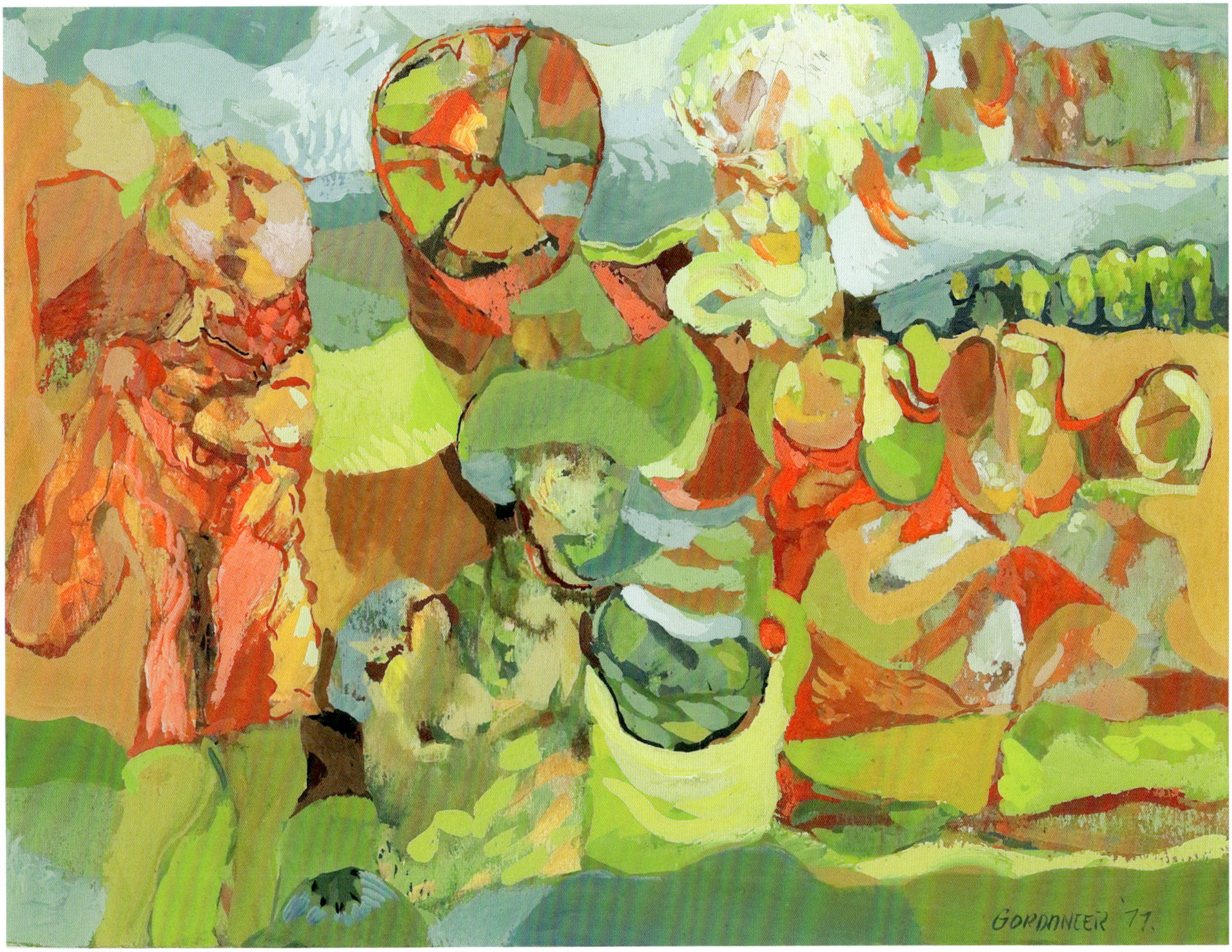

Picnic, 1977, gouache on board

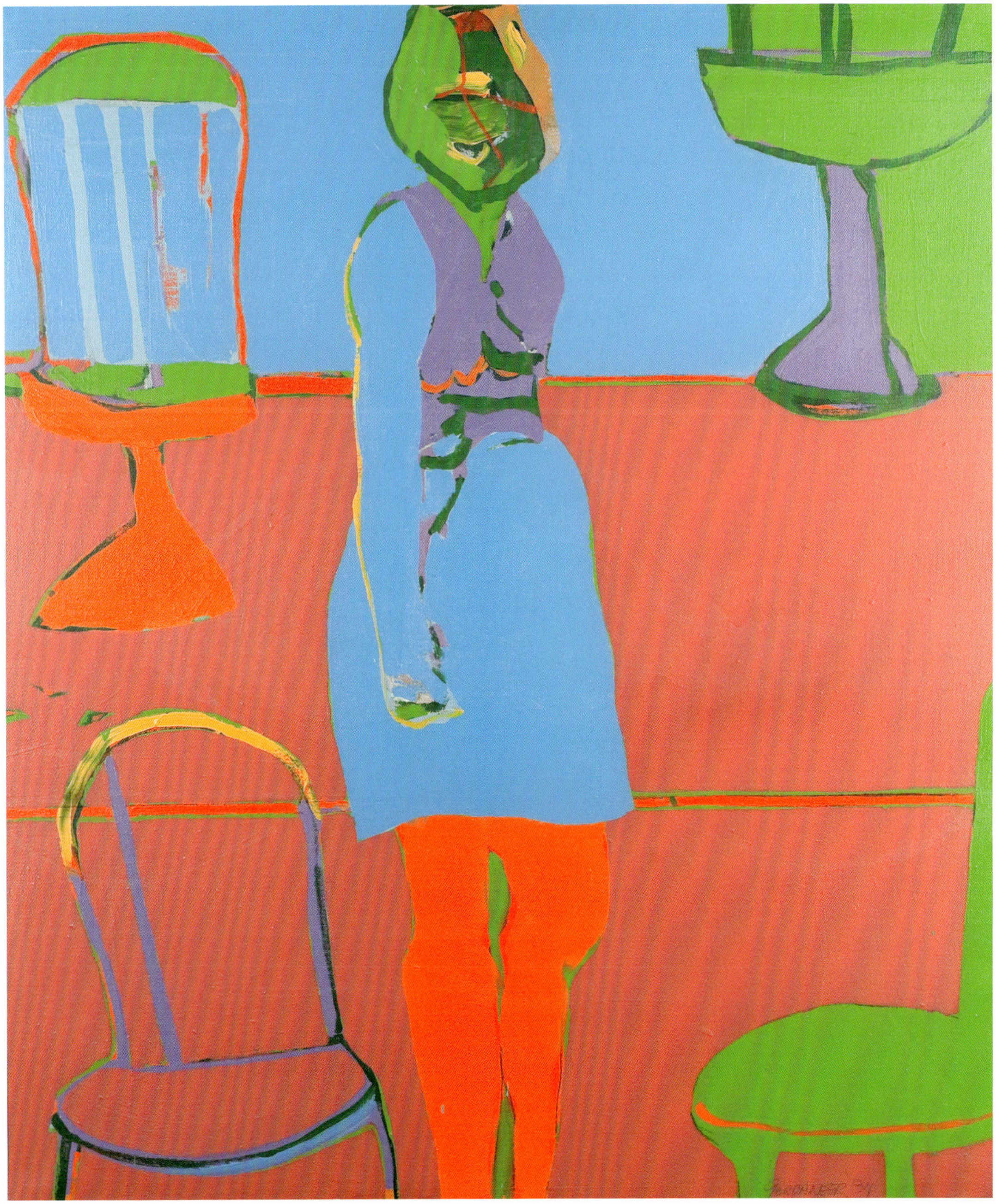

Waitress II, 1984, acrylic on canvas

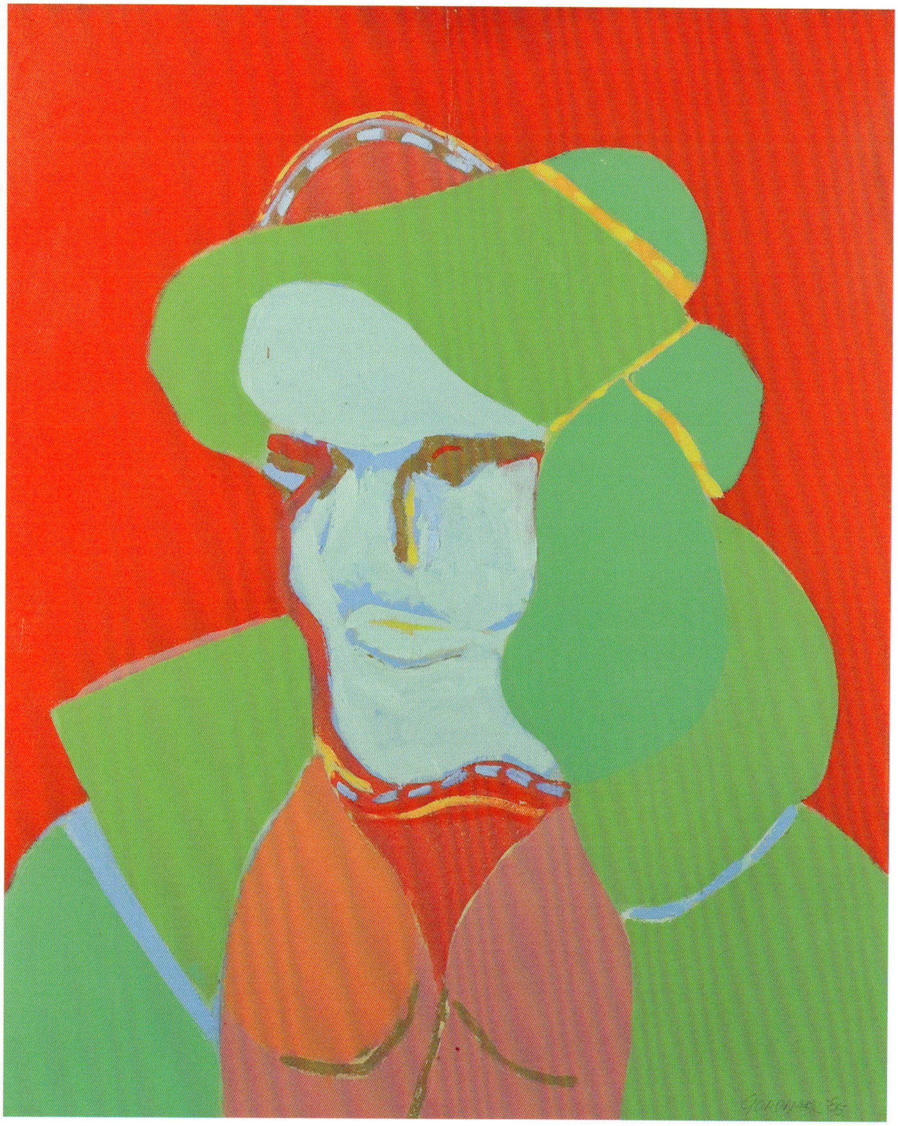

Hortense, 1985, oil on canvas

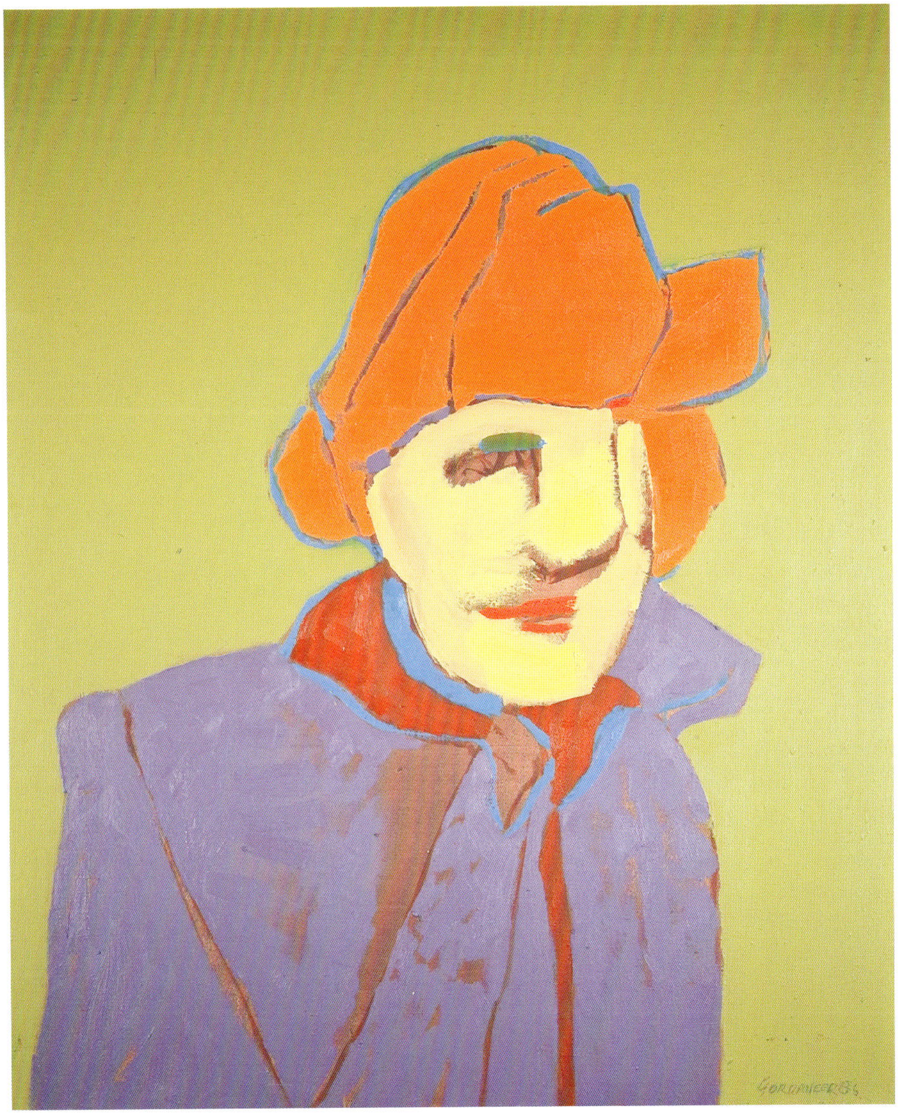

Rufus, 1986, oil on canvas

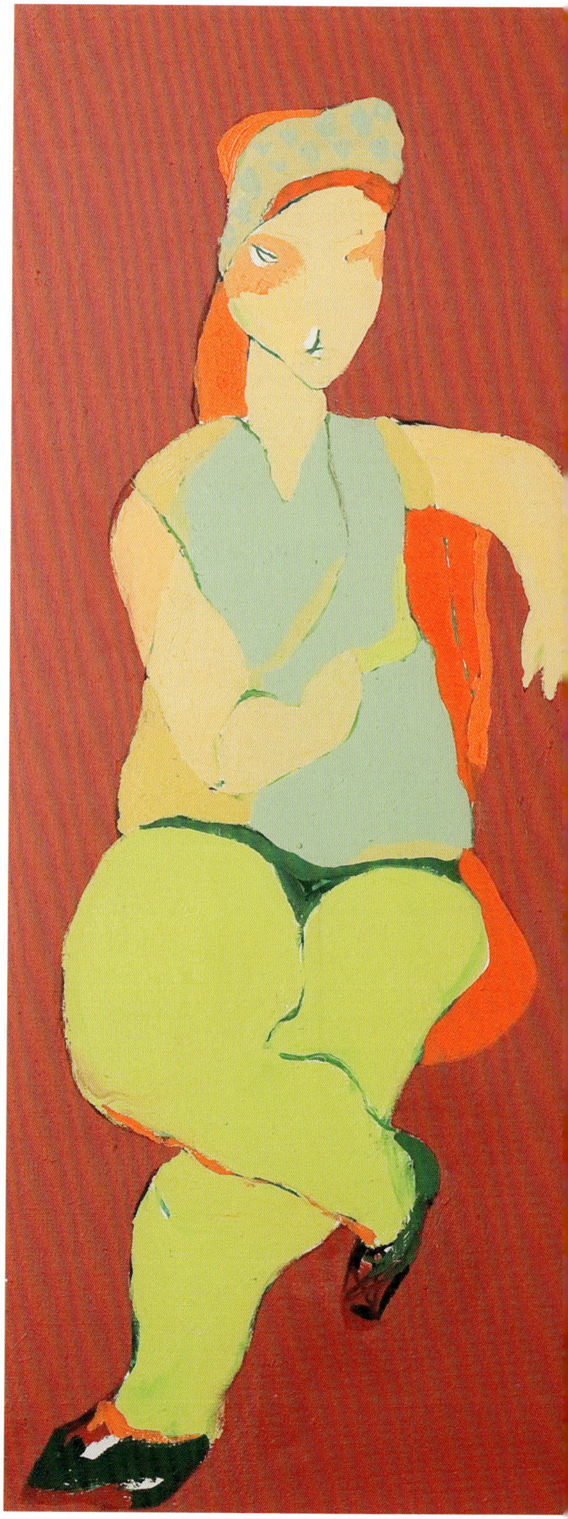

Three Sisters (triptych), 1986, oil on canvas

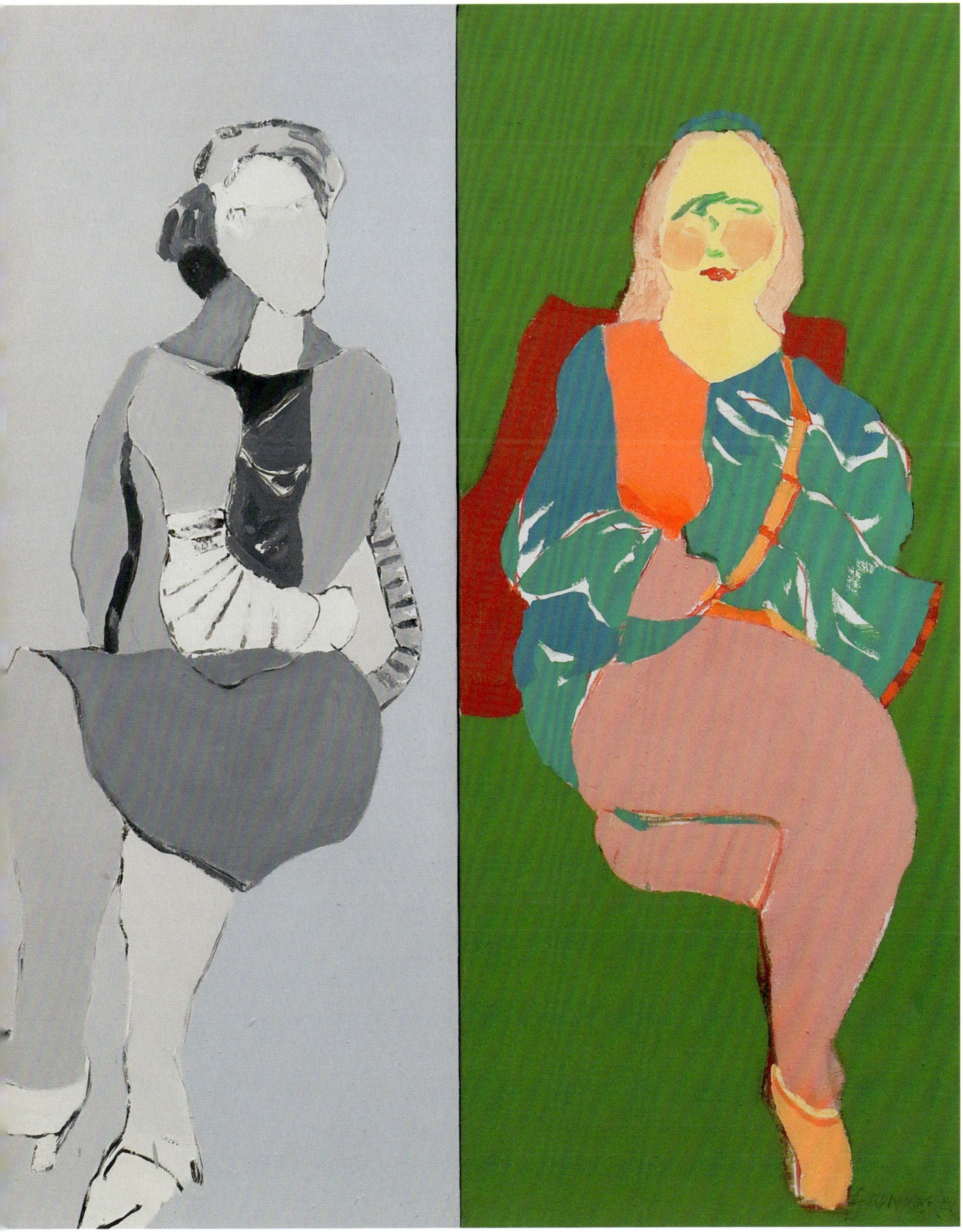

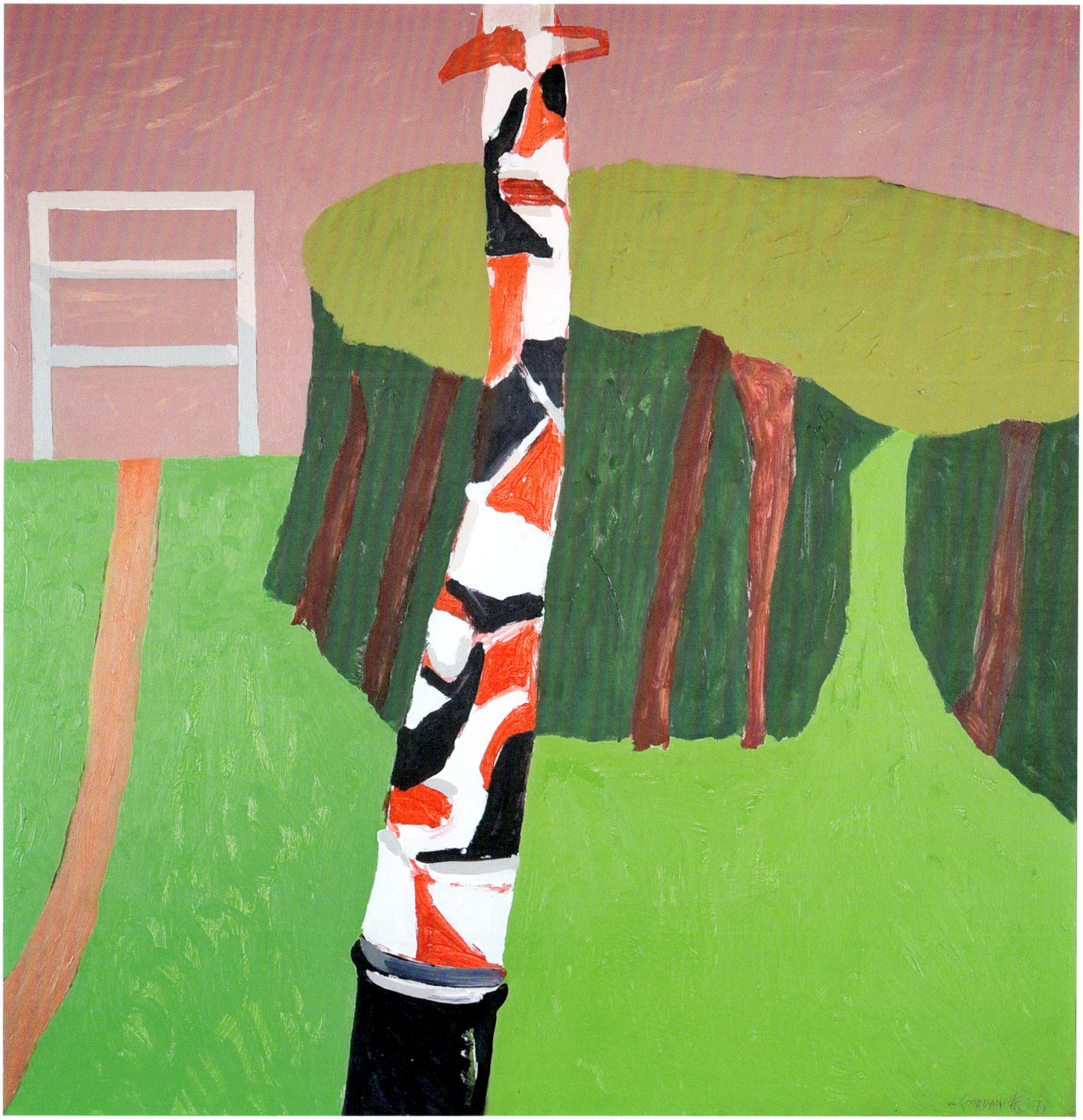

Beacon Hill Series: Totem, 1987, oil on panel

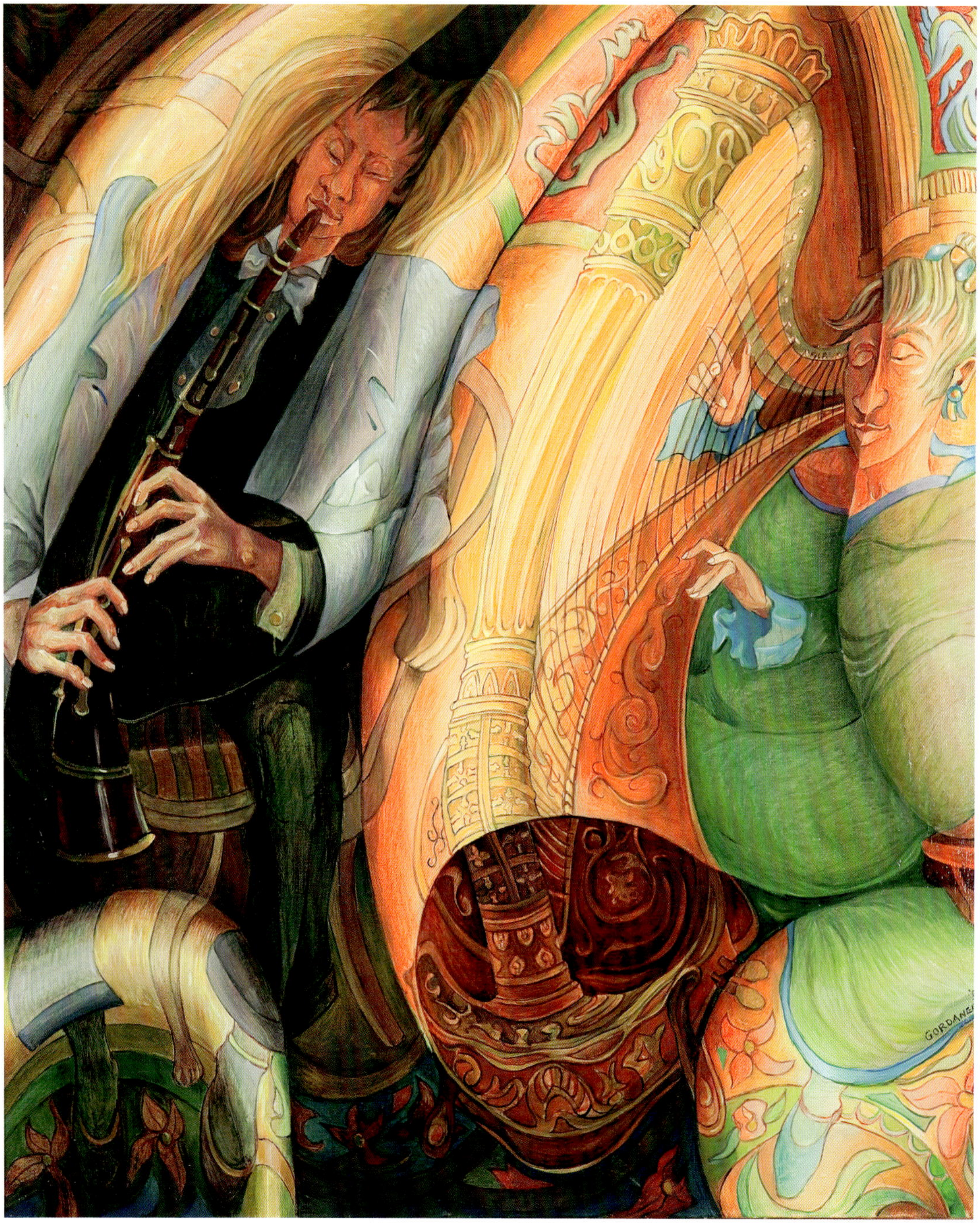

The Harpist, 1993, oil on canvas

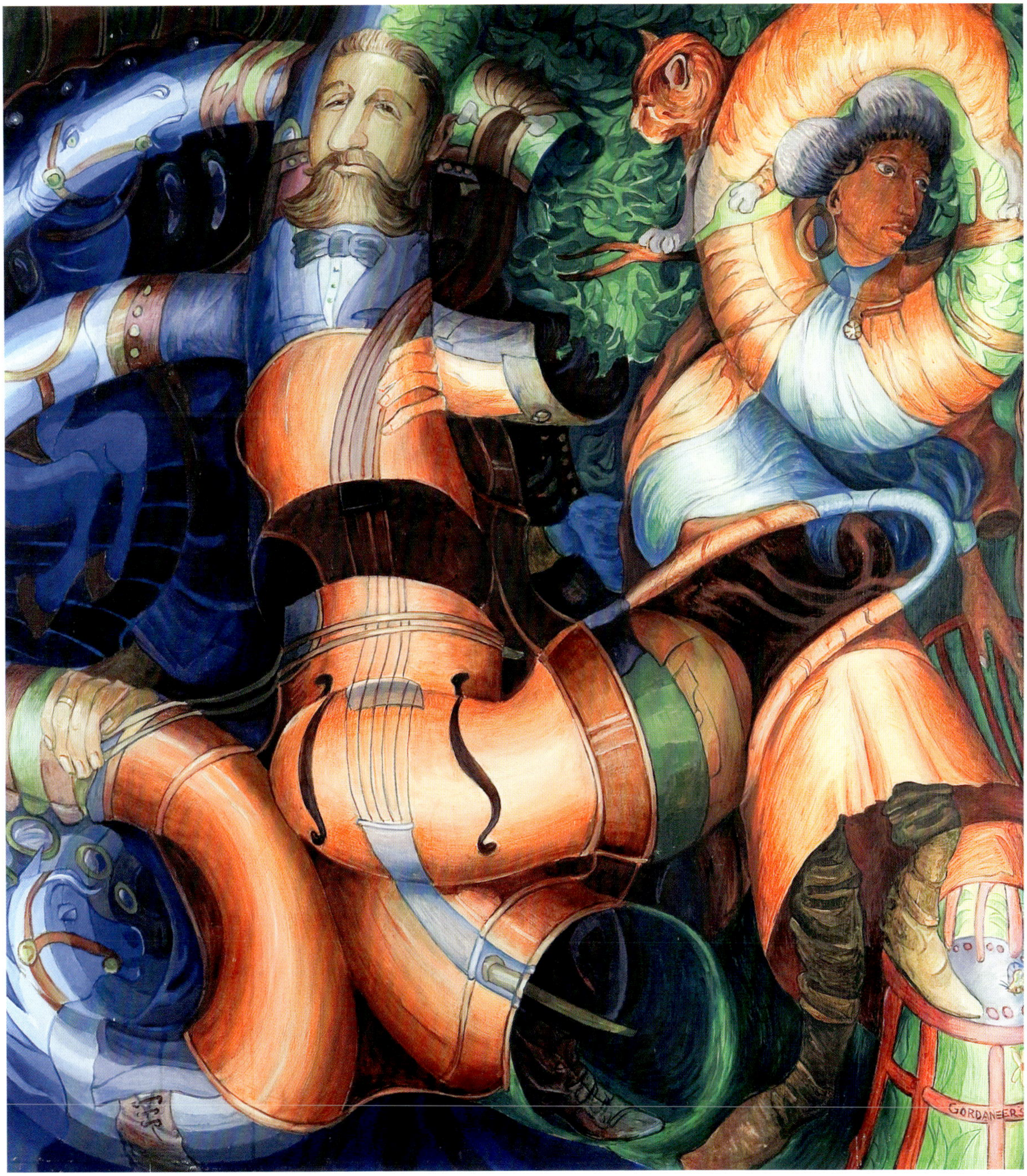

Bass Players and Violinists, 1993, oil on canvas

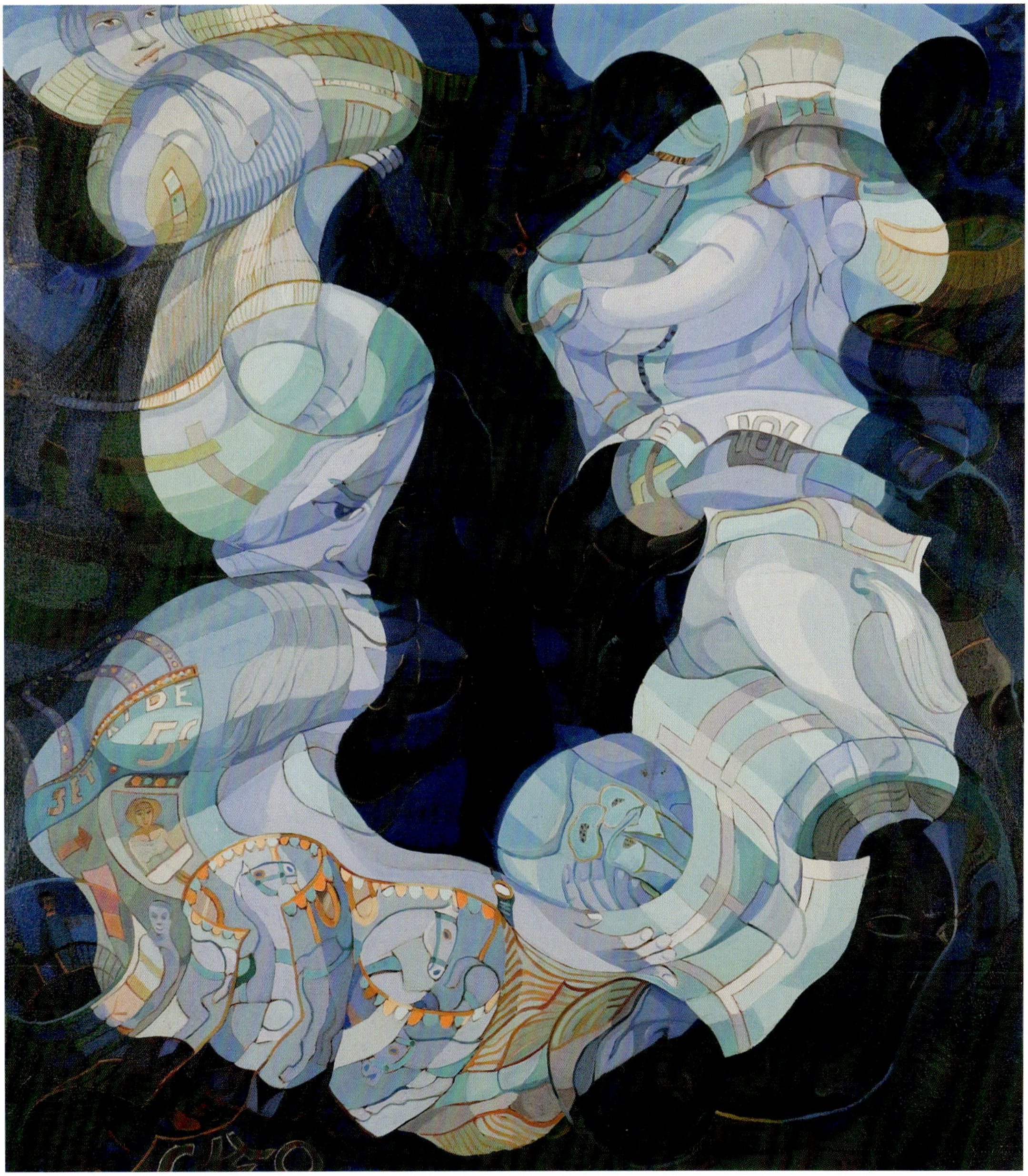

Licence, 1993, oil on canvas

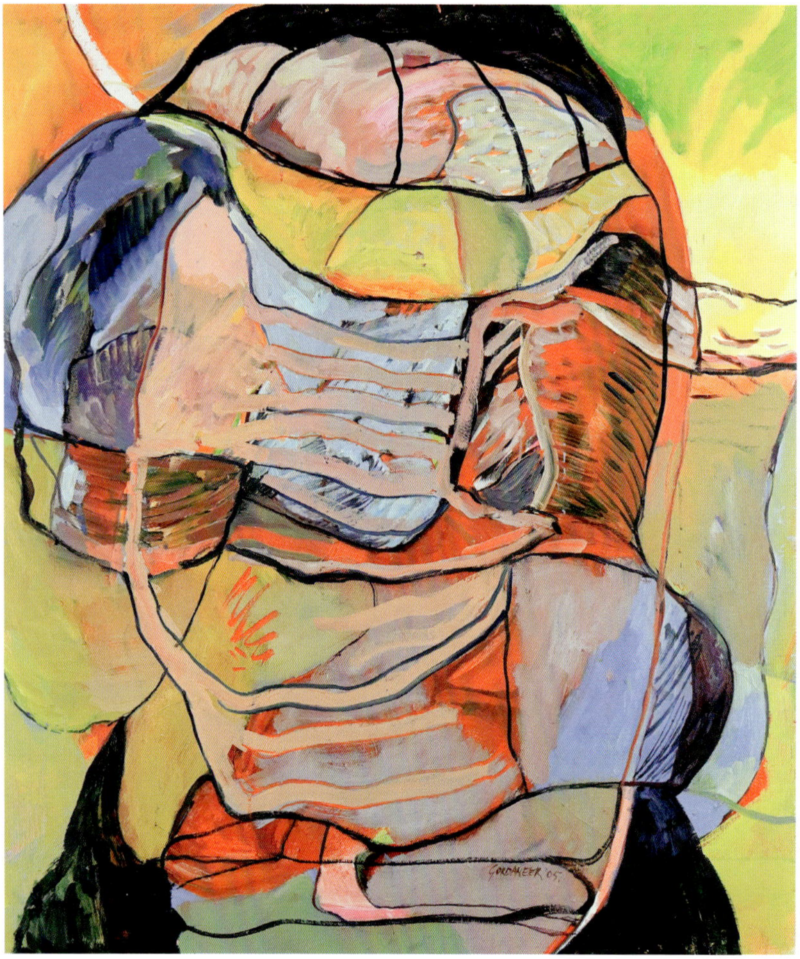

The Umpire, 2005, oil on panel

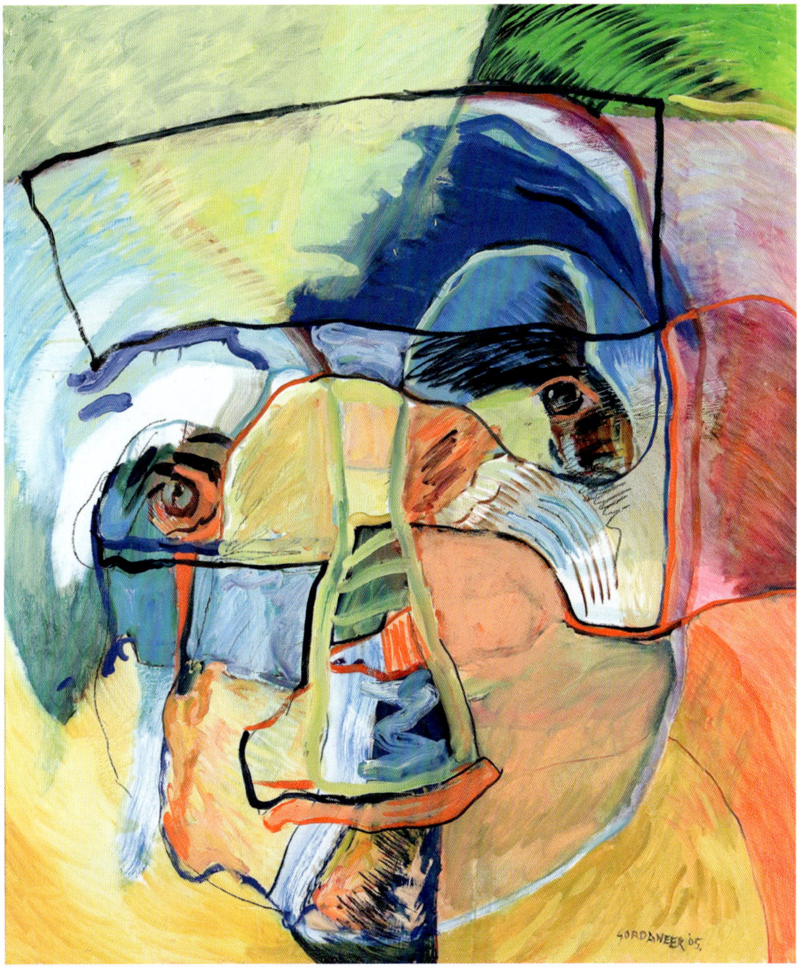

Sailor, 2005, oil on panel

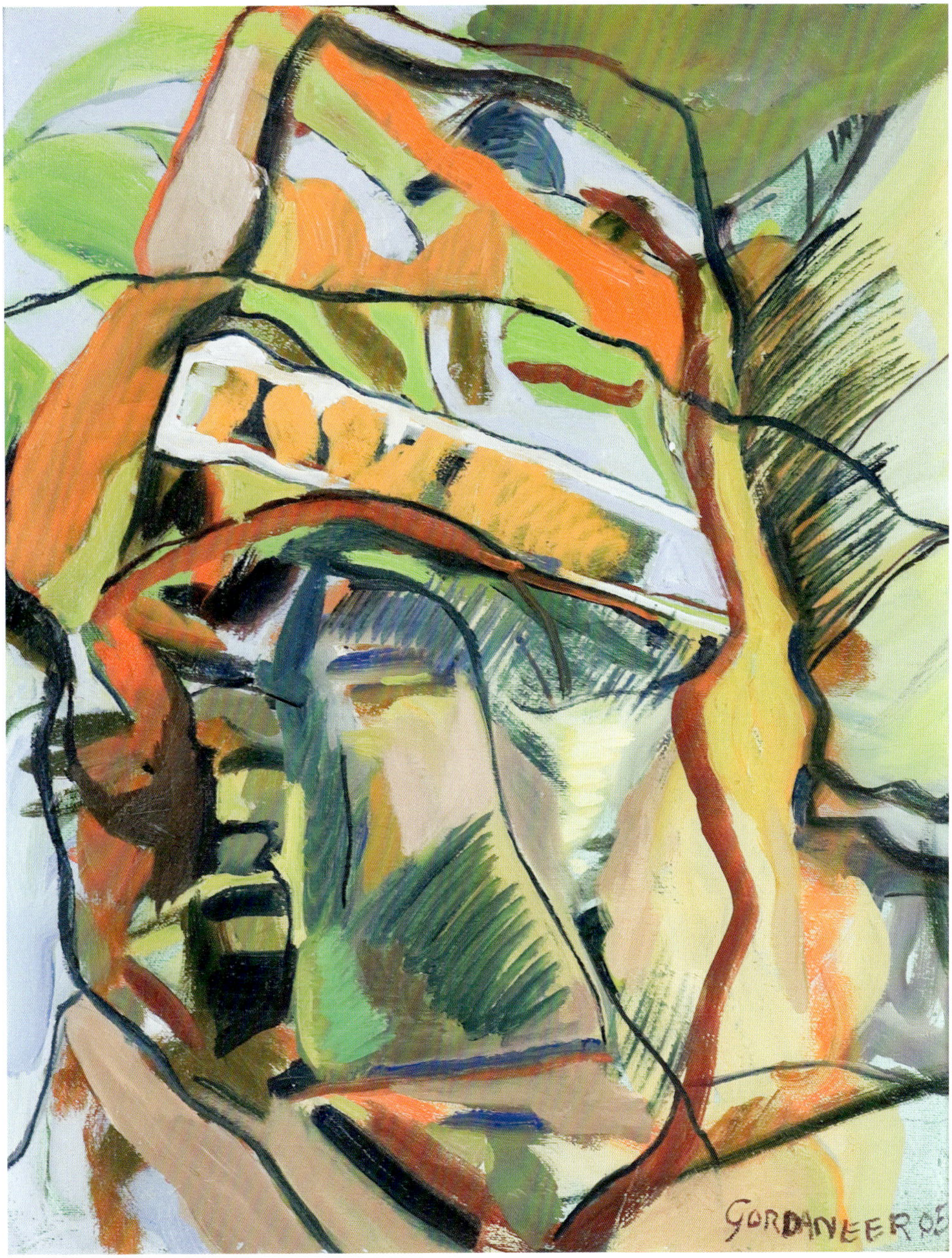

Gumshoe, 2005, oil on canvas

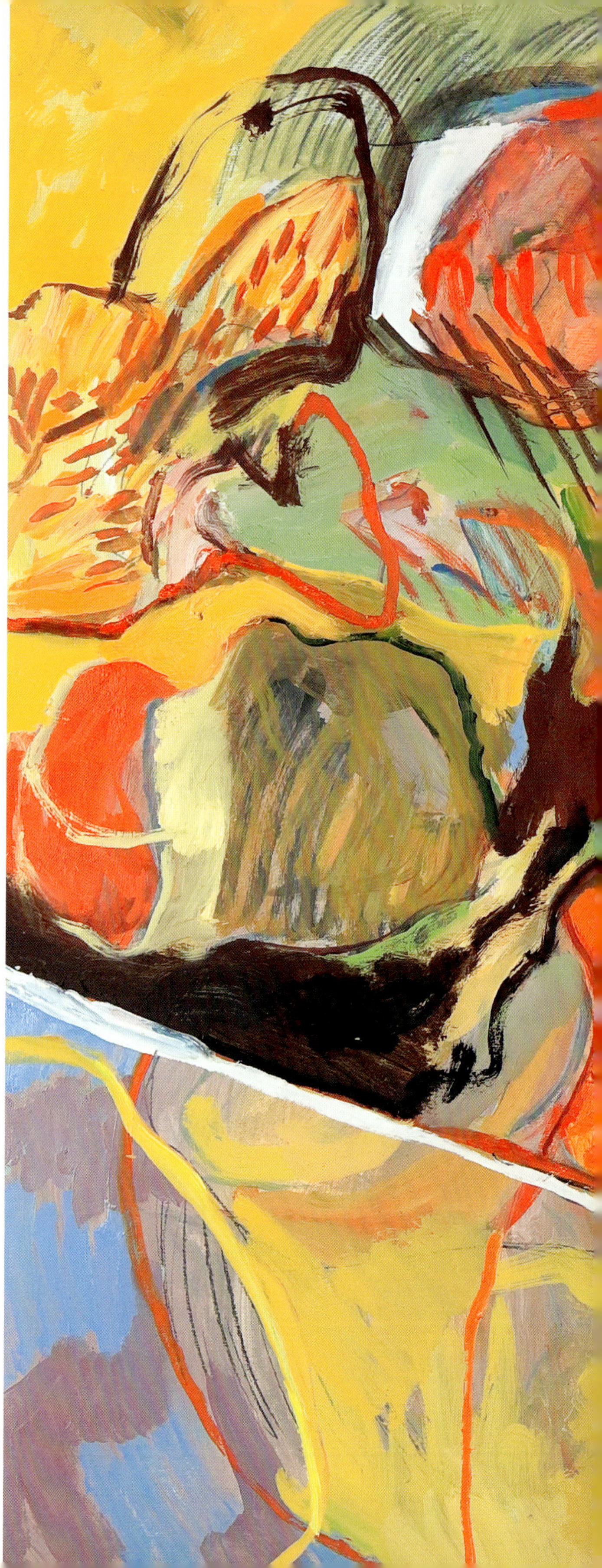

Ship of Fools, 2009, oil on panel

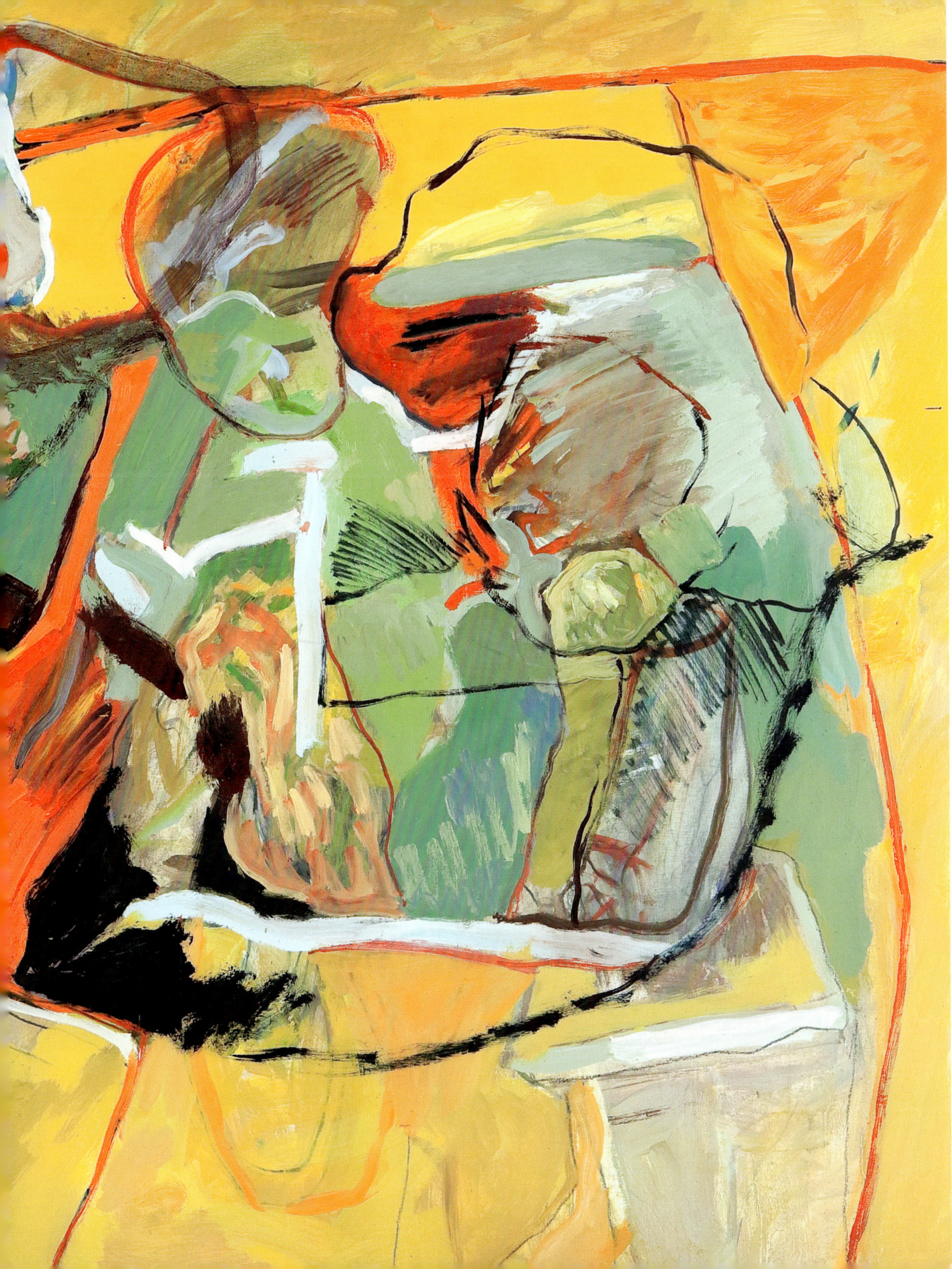

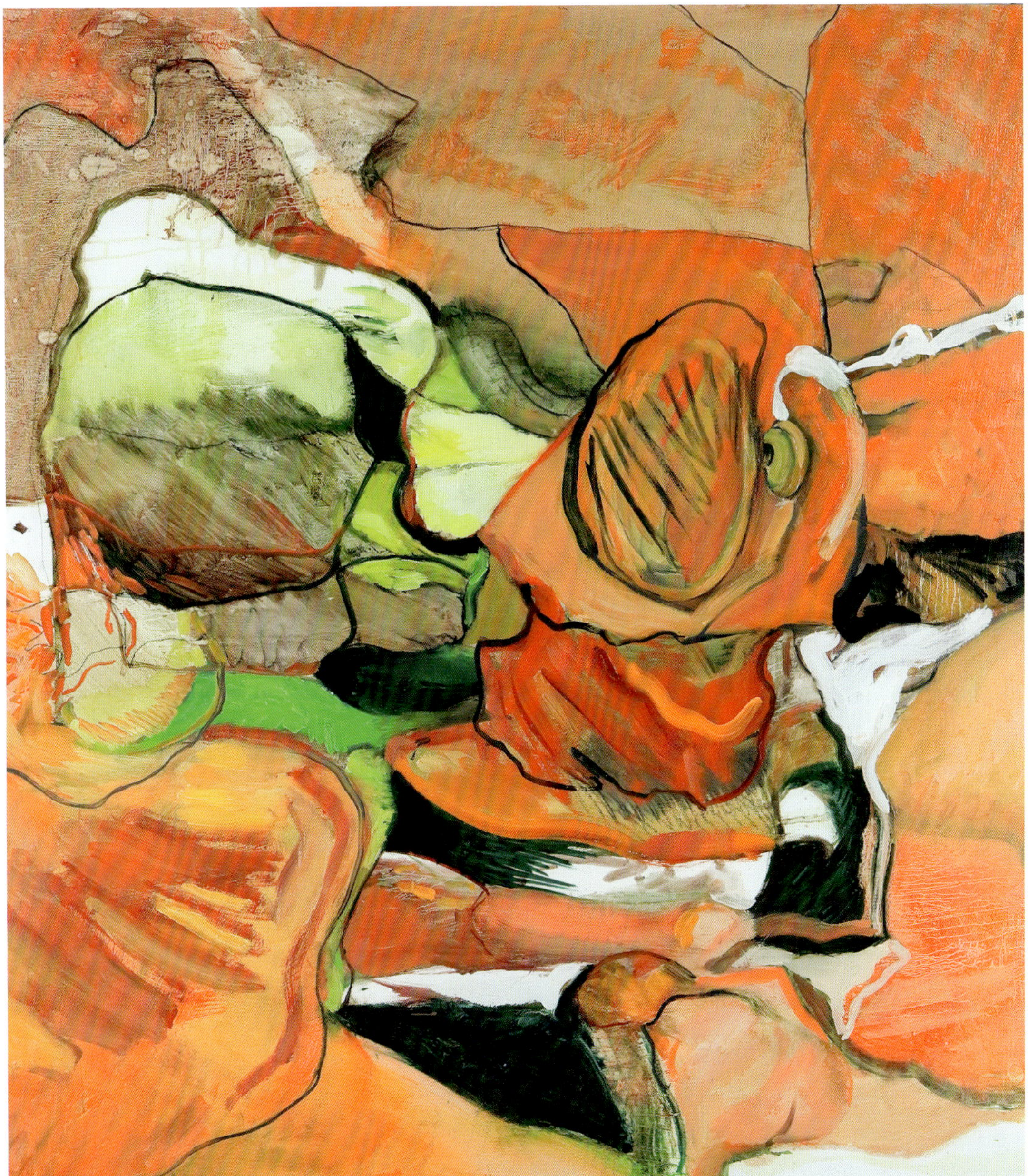

The Parlour, 2009, oil on panel

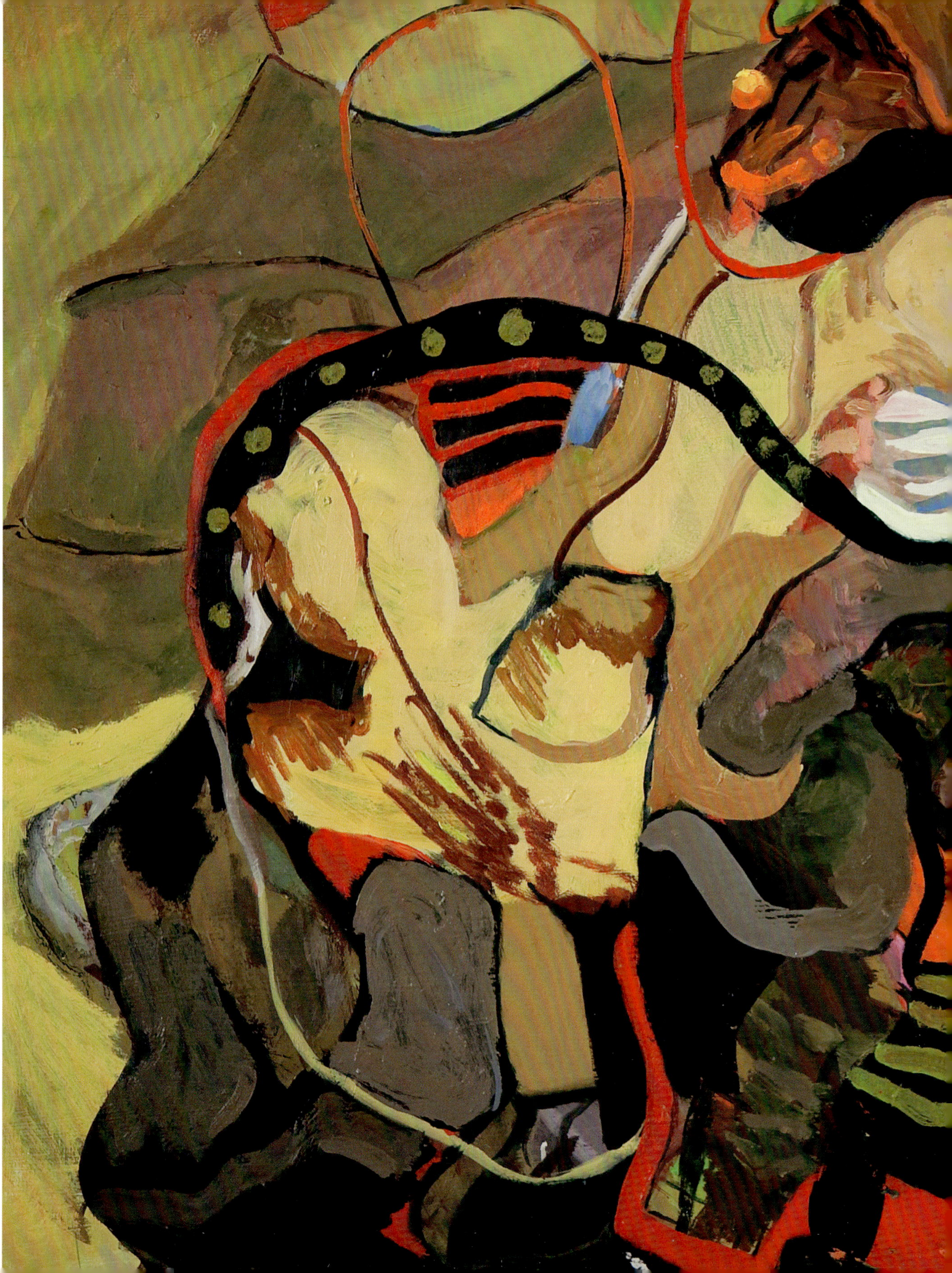

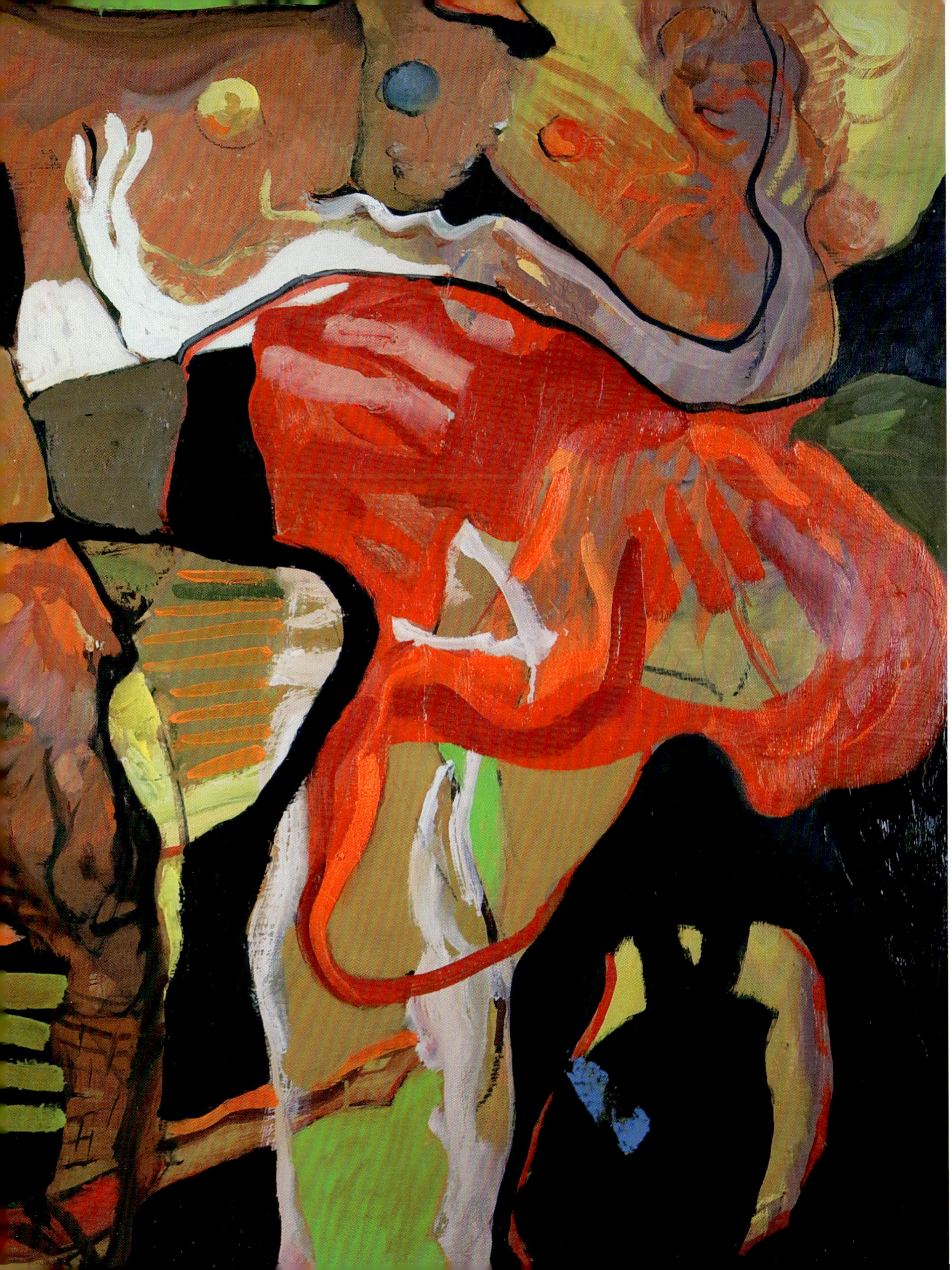

PREVIOUS SPREAD: **Send in the Clowns**, 2009, oil on panel

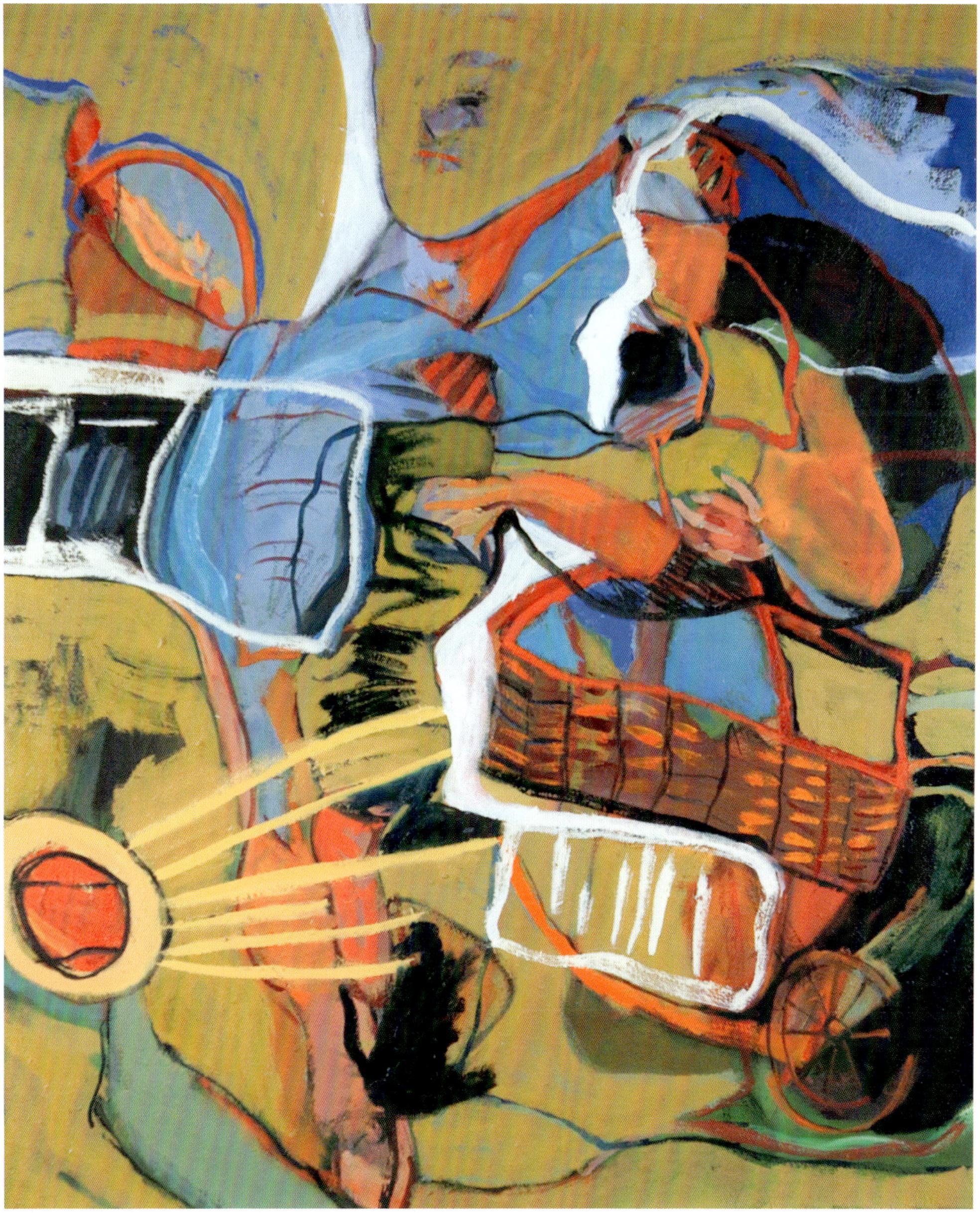

To the Park, 2009, oil on canvas

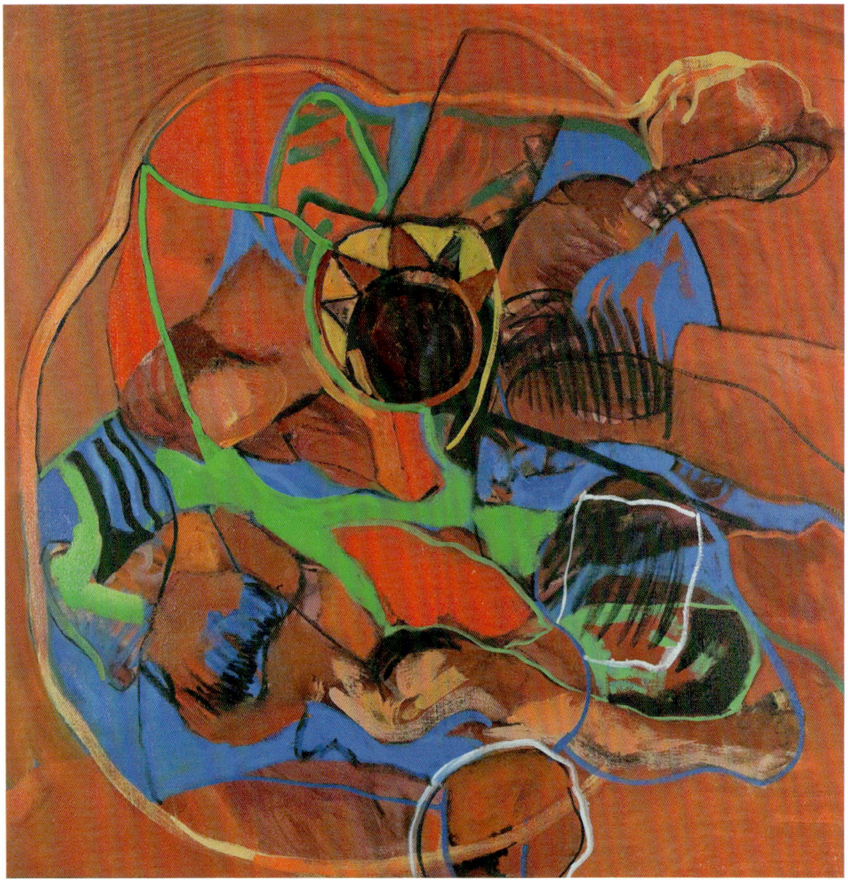

The Sign, 2009, oil on panel

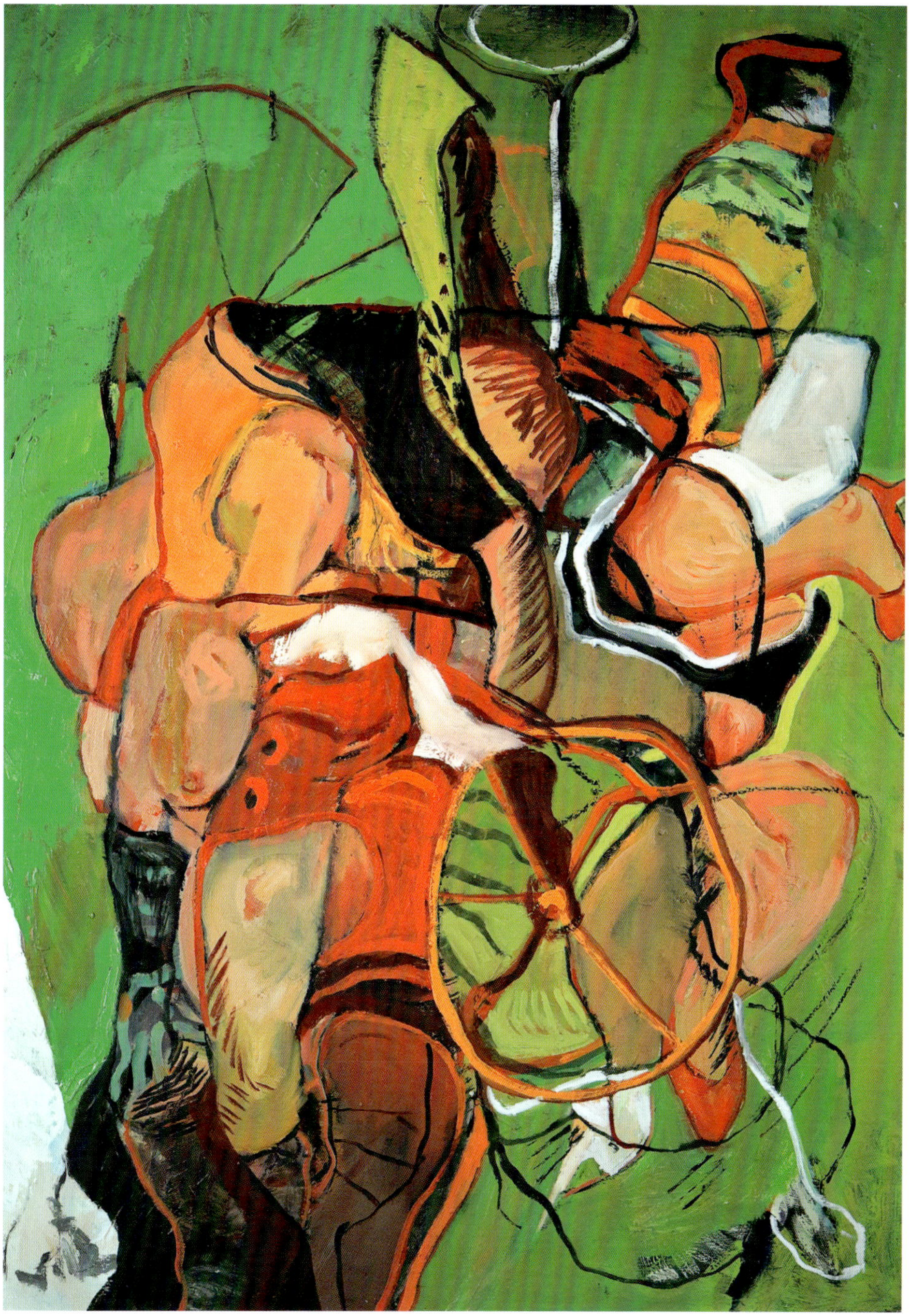

They All Came Tumbling Down, 2009, oil on panel

Sketches

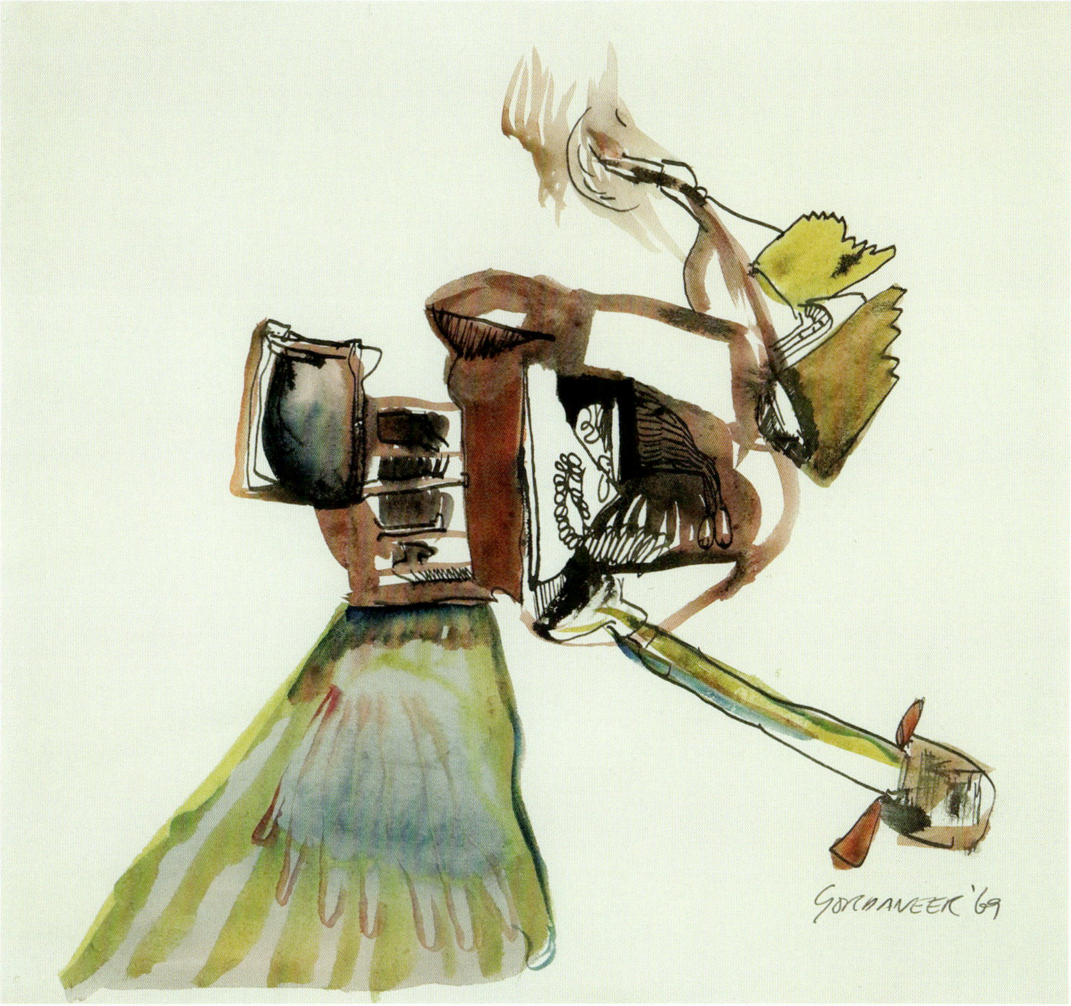

Antique Outboard, 1969, pen and watercolour on paper

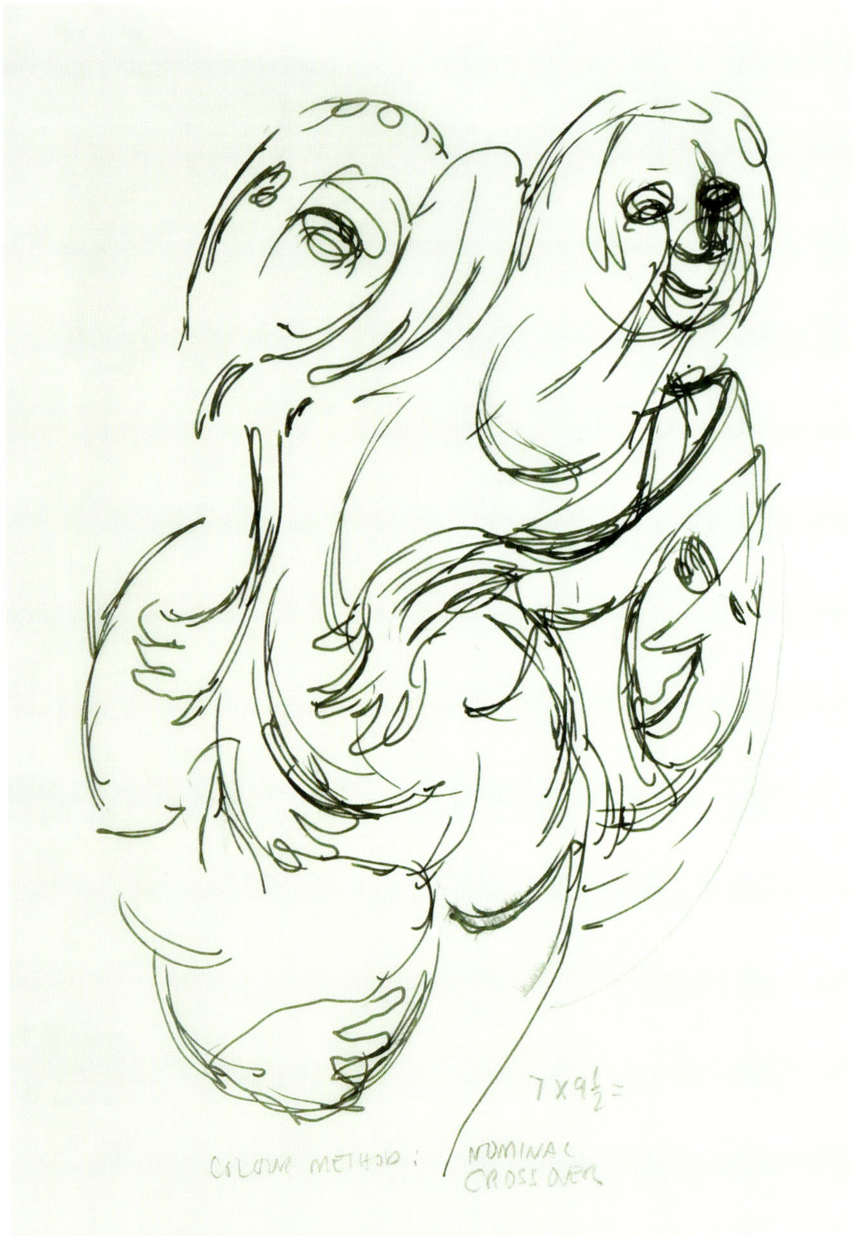

Topological Study (detail), c.1990s, ink on paper

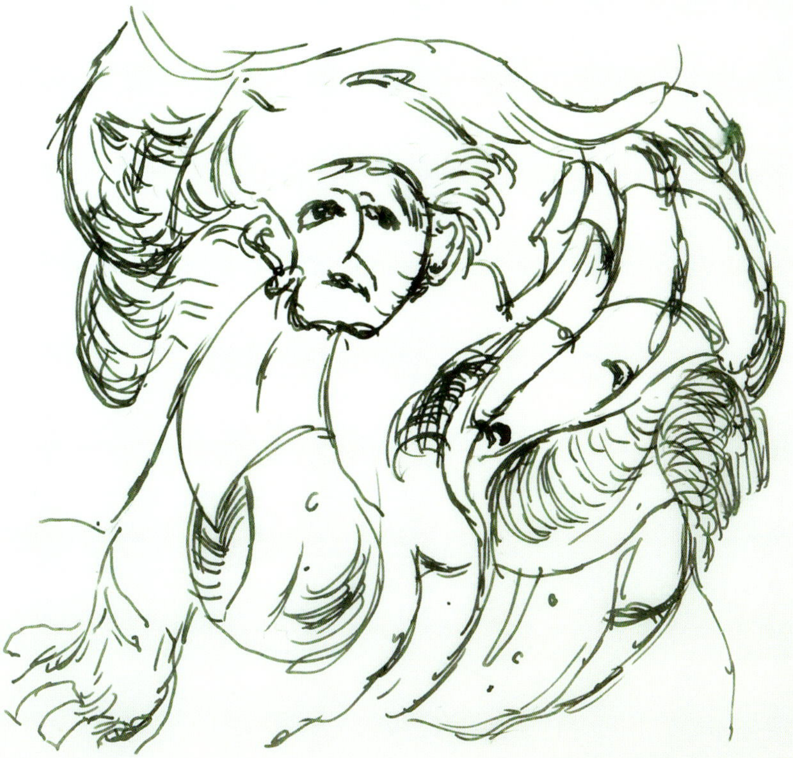

Topological Study (detail), c.1990s, ink on paper

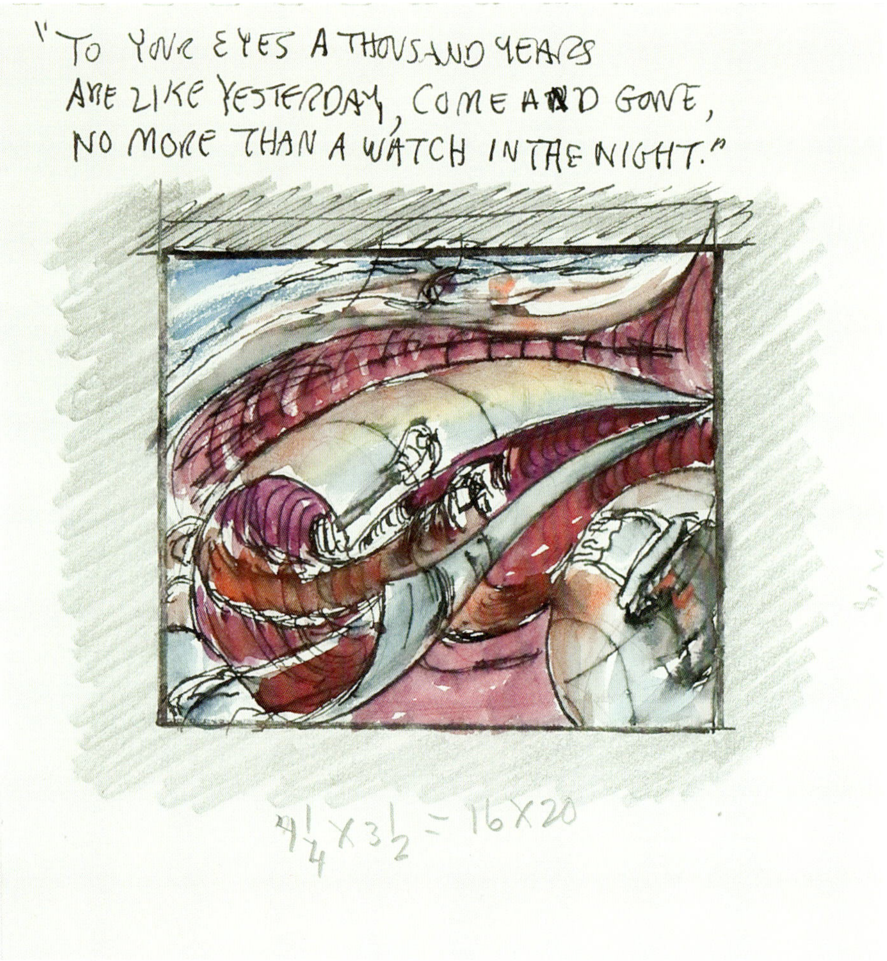

Topological study for poem #1, 1997, pencil, watercolour on paper

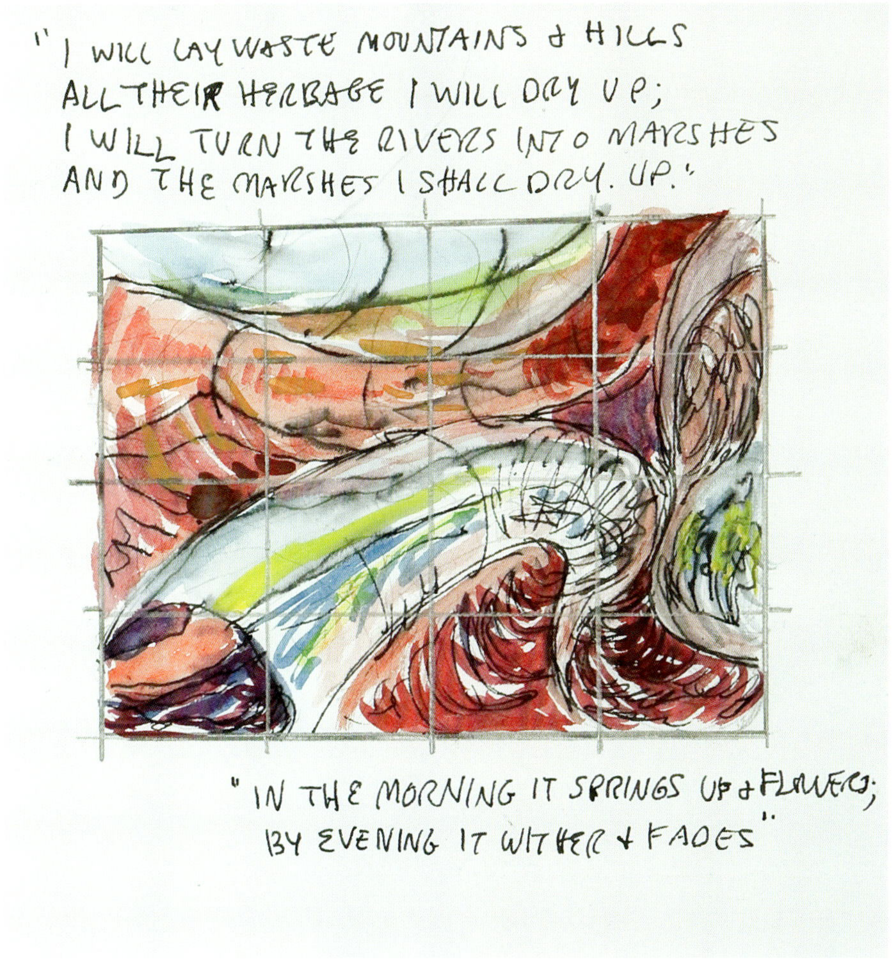

Topological study for poem #2, 1997, pencil, watercolour on paper

List of Works • James Gordaneer b. 1933 Canadian

Barns, Whitney ON, 1953
oil on masonite
40.5 x 51 cm
Collection of the Artist

New York Subway, 1953
oil on masonite
40.5 x 58.5 cm
Collection of the Artist

Orrie's Place, Whitney ON, 1953
oil on masonite
40.5 x 51 cm
Collection of the Artist

Circus — Between Acts, 1954
oil on masonite
30.5 x 40.5 cm
Collection of the Artist

Clown, 1955
oil on masonite
61 x 46 cm
Collection of the Artist

Greek Collage, 1967
newsprint, glue,
and ink on paper
33 x 25 cm
Collection of the Artist

Space Station, 1969
acrylic on canvas
63.5 x 152.5 cm
Collection of Marc Christensen

Palaeo Plain, 1970
acrylic on canvas
122 x 165 cm
Collection of the Artist

Sofa, 1971
oil on canvas
122 x 140 cm
Collection of the Artist

Space Odyssey, 1972
oil on linen
91.5 x 91.5 cm
Collection of the Artist

Spring Occurrence, 1973
oil on canvas
91.5 x 104 cm
Collection of the Artist

Pineapples and Eggplant, 1974
oil on linen
61 x 103 cm
Collection of the Artist

Atrium in Hades, 1976
oil on linen
86 x 91.5 cm
Collection of the Artist

Enigma, 1976
oil on linen
40.5 x 40.5 cm
Collection of the Artist

Picnic, 1977
gouache on board
25.5 x 30.5 cm
Collection of the Artist

Washing Her Hair, 1977
oil on canvas
46 x 40.5 cm
Collection of Alisa Gordaneer

Arbutus Cove, 1978
oil on linen
68.5 x 89 cm
Collection of the Artist

Waitress II, 1984
acrylic on canvas
131 x 112 cm
Collection of the Artist

Circus Series: Slack Wire, 1985
oil on canvas
135 x 104 cm
Collection of the Artist

Hortense, 1985
oil on canvas
109 x 91.5 cm
Collection of the Artist

Rufus, 1986
oil on canvas
109 x 91.5 cm
Collection of the Artist

Three Sisters (triptych), 1986
oil on canvas
110 x 139 cm
Collection of the Artist

Beacon Hill Series: Band Stand, 1987
oil on panel
91.5 x 91.5 cm
Collection of the Artist

Beacon Hill Series: Totem, 1987
oil on panel
91.5 x 91.5 cm
Collection of the Artist

Bass Players and Violinists, 1993
oil on canvas
100 x 110 cm
Collection of Lynda and
Alan Cassels

The Harpist, 1993
oil on canvas
94 x 112 cm
Collection of Lynda and
Alan Cassels

Licence, 1993
oil on canvas
152 x 138 cm
Collection of the Artist

Gumshoe, 2005
oil on canvas
51 x 41 cm
Collection of the Artist

Sailor, 2005
oil on panel
107 x 91.5 cm
Collection of the Artist

The Umpire, 2005
oil on panel
107 x 91.5 cm
Collection of the Artist

The Parlour, 2009
oil on panel
91.5 x 107 cm
Collection of the Artist

Send in the Clowns, 2009
oil on panel
81 x 122 cm
Collection of the Artist

Ship of Fools, 2009
oil on panel
107 x 91.5 cm
Private Collection

The Sign, 2009
oil on panel
107 x 91.5 cm
Collection of the Artist

Summer Sky, Deep Woods, 2009
oil on panel
107 x 91.5 cm
Collection of the Artist

They All Came Tumbling Down, 2009
oil on panel
109 x 79 cm
Collection of the Artist

To the Park, 2009
oil on canvas
91.5 x 76 cm
Collection of the Artist

SKETCHES

Baldwin St., 1959
pencil on paper
23.5 x 30 cm
Collection of the Artist

Abstraction of Baldwin St., 1959
pencil on paper
22.5 x 30.5 cm
Collection of the Artist

Antique Outboard, 1969
pen and watercolour on paper
27.5 x 38 cm
Collection of the Artist

Roller Derby, 1971
pen and watercolour on paper
30.5 x 22.5 cm
Collection of the Artist

Moss and Fairfield, c.1980s
pen and ink on paper
21.5 x 25 cm
Collection of the Artist

Studies of Concentration of Light, c.1990s
pencil, ink and watercolour on paper
14 x 28 cm
Collection of the Artist

Topological Study, c.1990s
ink on paper
28 x 14 cm
Collection of the Artist

Topological study for poem #1 and #2, 1997
pencil, watercolour on paper
27.5 x 35.5 cm
Collection of the Artist

James Gordaneer, RCA

Curriculum Vitae

1933 Born in Toronto, Ontario

1952–62 In lieu of formal education, travelled frequently to Mexico, France, Spain, Greece, Finland and other European countries

1976 Moved to Victoria, BC

1989–99 Co-founded the Chapman Group of Artists

2009 Currently represented by Fran Willis Gallery

Education

1952–55 Part-time work/study position at Doon School of Fine Arts.

Took courses with Jack Bechtel, Carl Schaefer, Yvonne Housser, Jock MacDonald, R. York Wilson and Leonard Brooks among others.

Selected Gallery Exhibitions

2006 Fran Willis Gallery, Victoria, BC: *Heads* (solo exhibition)

Heads exhibition travelled to:
Grand Forks Art Gallery, Grand Forks, BC
Castlegar Art Gallery, Castlegar, BC
Penticton Art Gallery, Penticton, BC

2004 Robert McLaughlin Gallery, Oshawa, ON: *James Gordaneer: Paintings from the 1950s and 1960s*

2003–04 Fran Willis Gallery, Victoria, BC

2003–04 Chapman West Fine Art, Victoria, BC

2002 Fran Willis Gallery, Victoria, BC: *Out of the Shadow* (solo exhibition)

2001 Chapman West Fine Art, Victoria, BC

2000 Chapman West Fine Art, Victoria, BC

1998 McPherson Library Gallery, University of Victoria, Victoria, BC

1995 Winchester Galleries, Victoria, BC

1989 North Park Gallery, Victoria, BC

1987 Art Gallery of Greater Victoria, Victoria, BC: *James Gordaneer: The Circus Series*

Threshold Gallery, Vancouver, BC

1986 Fine Arts Center, Washington State University, Pullman, WA

1984 North Park Gallery, Victoria, BC

Gadatsy Gallery, Toronto, ON

1982 Kyle's Gallery, Victoria, BC

1980 Kyle's Gallery, Victoria, BC

1979 Gustaffson Gallery, Brampton, ON

1978 Kyle's Gallery, Victoria, BC

Merton Gallery, Toronto, ON

1977 Merton Gallery, Toronto, ON

Utley's Gallery, Victoria, BC

1974 Trent University, Peterborough, ON

Merton Gallery, Toronto, ON

Gustaffson Gallery, Brampton, ON

Gadatsy Gallery, Toronto, ON

1973 Merton Gallery, Toronto, ON

1972 Gallery 33, Bath, ON

1971 University of Waterloo, Waterloo, ON

Robert McLaughlin Gallery, Oshawa, ON

Utley's Gallery, Victoria, BC

1969 Sheridan College, Oakville, ON

1966 Albert White Gallery, Toronto, ON

1964 Penthouse Gallery, Montreal, PQ

1961 Upstairs Gallery, Toronto, ON

Penthouse Gallery, Montreal, PQ

1956 Doon School Gallery, Doon, ON

Selected Group Exhibitions

2009 Mercurio Gallery, Victoria, BC

2007 Peterborough Art Gallery, Peterborough, ON: *Recent Work: John Climenhage, Jeremy Gordaneer, James Gordaneer*

2002 Chapman West Fine Art, Victoria, BC

2001 Chapman West Fine Art, Victoria, BC

2000 Chapman West Fine Art, Victoria, BC

1999 Chapman House, Victoria, BC

Zeitgeist Gallery, Detroit, MI

Eaton's Centre, Victoria, BC: *Chiapas Liberation Theology in Art*

1998 Homer Watson Gallery, Doon, ON: *Doon School Fiftieth Anniversary*

Chapman House, Victoria, BC

UBC Festival of Strings, University of British Columbia, Vancouver, BC, Chapman Group

Michelle Frost Gallery, Victoria, BC: *RCA Victoria Members*

1988 The Victoria College of Art Gallery, Victoria, BC

1986 Art Gallery of Greater Victoria, Victoria, BC: *Art in Victoria: 1960–1986*

North Park Gallery, Victoria, BC

Maltwood Art Museum and Gallery, University of Victoria, Victoria, BC: *RCA Exhibition*

1980 George Williams Art Gallery, Concordia University, Montreal, PQ

Agnes Etherington Art Centre, Queen's University, Kingston, ON: *Other Realities: The Legacy of Surrealism in Canadian Art*

Other Realities exhibition travelled to: Centre Culturel Canadien, Paris, France

Canada House, London, UK

1979 Equinox Gallery, Vancouver, BC

1975 Art Gallery of Ontario, Toronto, ON: *Chairs Exhibition*

1974 Saidye Bronfman Centre, Montreal, PQ: *Drawing Rediscovered*

1972 Albright Knox Art Museum, Buffalo, NY: *Canadian Painters*

1966 Canadian Group of Painters, Montreal, PQ

Hamilton Winter Show, Hamilton, ON

1965 Jerrold Morris Gallery, Toronto, ON

Toronto Art Gallery, Toronto, ON: *Ontario Society of Artists*

1964 Canadian Group of Painters, Montreal, PQ

1963 The Vincent Price Collection

1962 Hamilton Winter Show, Hamilton, ON

Montreal Museum of Fine Arts, Montreal, PQ: *Montreal Spring Show*

1961 National Gallery, Ottawa, ON: *IV Biennial*

Selected Collections

Art Gallery of Greater Victoria, Victoria, BC

Canada Council Art Bank

Concordia University, Montreal, PQ

Crown Life, Toronto, ON

Dow Chemical, Sarnia, ON

Esso Collection, Calgary, AB

Homer Watson Gallery, Doon, ON

Imperial Oil, Toronto and Sarnia, ON

McMichael Canadian Art Collection, Kleinburg, ON

Michael Williams Collection, University of Victoria, Victoria, BC

Peel Region Art Museum, Brampton, ON

Prince George Art Gallery, Prince George, BC

Queen's University, Kingston, ON

Robert McLaughlin Art Gallery, Oshawa, ON

Sarnia Art Gallery, Sarnia, ON

Sir George Williams University, Montreal, PQ

University of Victoria, Victoria, BC

and numerous private collections

Societies and Groups

Canadian Group of Painters

Chapman Group of Artists

Ontario Society of Artists

Royal Canadian Academy of Arts

Canadian Society of Painters in Watercolour

Teaching

1955–2004 Numerous workshops, seminars and private lessons

1991–95 Metchosin International Summer School of the Arts, Metchosin, BC

1977–92 Victoria College of Art, Victoria, BC

1976–79 Camosun College, Victoria, BC

1966–69 Orangeville District High School, Orangeville, ON

1959–65 Central Technical School, Toronto, ON

1956–59 University of Toronto, School of Architecture, Toronto, ON

1955–61 Doon School of Fine Arts, Doon, ON

Selected Articles and Reviews

Amos, Robert. "Not Too Quotable." *Times Colonist* (Victoria, BC), 11 March 1989, p. C2.

"Three Rings of Fun on View at the Art Gallery." *Times Colonist* (Victoria, BC), 2 February 1987, p. C4.

Ayer, Robert. "Artists in Contrast at Two Exhibitions." *Montreal Star*, 16 April 1964.

Boughner, Jacqueline. Interview with James Gordaneer. Exhibition Catalogue, Robert McLaughlin Gallery, Oshawa, ON, 1971.

Davidson, Liane. "James Gordaneer: The Circus Series." Exhibition Catalogue, Art Gallery of Greater Victoria, Victoria, BC, 1987.

Kerr, Darlene, Victoria Baker and Kevin McLaughlin. *Doon School of Fine Arts (1948–1966)*. Homer Watson House and Gallery, Kitchener, ON, 1988.

Kritzweiser, Kay. "Rustic Life Influence on Gordaneer Painting." *The Globe and Mail* (Toronto, ON), 19 October 1971, p. 23.

Leach, David. "The Rise and Fall of the House of Chapman." *Monday Magazine* (Victoria, BC), 1 April 1999, pp. 7–8.

Little, Barbara. "Art in Victoria 'Who's Who' of Canadian Art." *Victoria Star* (Victoria, BC), 27 August 1986, p. 7.

McCarthy, Pearl. "The Younger Set Are Finding a Thrill on Top." *The Globe and Mail* (Toronto, ON), 14 July 1956, p. 4.

Nowosad, Frank. "James Gordaneer: The Urge to Simply Paint." *Monday Magazine* (Victoria, BC), 10 April 1978, p. 19.

Sanroman, Lucia. *Embedded Conflict in the Work of James Gordaneer*. Master's thesis, University of Victoria, 2003.

Thorne, Barry. "Spring Exhibition: Pieces are NOW Oriented." *Kingston Whig-Standard* (Kingston, ON), 18 May 1972, p. 30.

Credits

Curator: Nicole Stanbridge

Guest Writer: Lisa Baldissera

Publication Project Manager: Nicole Stanbridge

Editor: Audrey McClellan

Publication Design: Frank Reimer

Photography: Stephen Topfer, Art Gallery of Greater Victoria

Printed in Canada by Friesens Corp.

Gallery Associates
ART GALLERY OF GREATER VICTORIA

British Columbia Arts Council
Supported by the Province of British Columbia

Canada Council for the Arts
Conseil des Arts du Canada

CRD
Making a difference...together

Art Gallery of Greater Victoria
1040 Moss Street
Victoria, British Columbia
Canada V8V 4P1
1.250.384.4101 aggv.bc.ca

Reference to Rhizome P. 28
33